Poetry Out Loud

POETRY OUT LOUD

EDITED BY ROBERT ALDEN RUBIN

WITH AN INTRODUCTION BY JAMES EARL JONES

Published by

ALGONQUIN BOOKS OF CHAPEL HILL

Post Office Box 2225

Chapel Hill, North Carolina   27515-2225

a division of

WORKMAN PUBLISHING COMPANY, INC.

708 Broadway

New York, New York 10003

Library of Congress Cataloging-in-Publication Data

Poetry out loud / edited by Robert Alden Rubin; with a introduction by James Earl Jones.

p.   cm.

"A burst of verses, from 'The waste land' to 'The owl and the pussy-cat,' with notes on how to recite them."

Includes bibliographical references and indexes.

ISBN 1-56512-030-2

1. English poetry. 2. American poetry. 3. Recitations.

I. Rubin, Robert Alden, 1958–

PR1175.P658   1993

821.008—dc20   93-3946 CIP

10 9 8 7 6 5 4 3 2 1

FIRST PRINTING

The editor would like to thank Penelope Niven, co-author with James Earl Jones of his forthcoming autobiography *James Earl Jones: Voices and Silences* (Scribners, 1993), for helping make possible Mr. Jones's introduction.

This book would not have been possible without the help of the many willing hands and generous imaginations at Algonquin Books of Chapel Hill and Workman Publishing. Thanks to Peter Workman, for taking a vague notion and giving it focus; to Shannon Ravenel for sticking up for it; to Elisabeth Scharlatt for working everything out; to Virginia Holman, for listening to poetry out loud over the room divider every morning; to Lisa Poteet, for diabolic advocacy; to Marjorie and Amy for close reading; to Ann, Kate, and all the others who suggested poems; to Ina, Ira, Lia, Julia, Sara, Linda, and everyone in sales, design, and production; to my many teachers over the years, who aren't to blame for mistakes, especially Phil Fitzpatrick, Galbraith Crump, John Rees Moore, and William Harmon. Most of all, to Cathy.

To LDR, for all the second chances

CONTENTS

INTRODUCTION
by James Earl Jones

First I would like to write for you a poem to be
*   shouted in the teeth of*
*   a strong wind.*
Next I would like to write one for you to sit on a
*   hill and read down the*
*   river valley on a late summer afternoon,*
*   reading it in less than a whisper . . .*
      —Carl Sandburg, "Horse Fiddle," *Smoke and Steel*

Poetry, like song, reverberates through centuries of time, echoing something primal and universal, akin to the grunts, growls, and trills of the Calibans and other creatures who spoke less than language but more than thought. Walt Whitman called it the "barbaric yawp." I believe language is an acquired intellectual exercise, while poetry and song are natural, primal expressions. Because poetry is primal, it is personal, a very subjective form, belonging to the inarticulate as well as the eloquent, the illiterate as well as the educated.

Poetry has always been a lifeline for me. When I was a

small boy, I began to stutter. From the time I was nearly six until I was about fourteen, I chose silence over speech. I retreated into muteness because my stuttering made speaking too difficult. But because I needed some way to express myself, even to myself, and to track the progress of my mind, I became a "closet" poet. I loved poetry, and began writing it myself.

In one of those fortunate accidents that can change lives, my high school English teacher in Brethren, Michigan, helped me to use poetry to reclaim my ability to speak. When Professor Donald Crouch discovered that I wrote poems, he asked to see some. One seemed to him good enough that he wondered if I might have plagiarized it. To defend myself, I had to read the poem aloud. Since I never spoke at school, this was an ordeal for me, but my honor was at stake. I had no choice but to stand up and read my poem to my teacher and classmates.

To my amazement and theirs, I read it without stumbling. That is how my teacher and I discovered that I did not stutter when I read the rhythmic *written* word aloud. It was no accident, then, that in the comfortable realm of the poetry I had written, expressing my own ideas and feelings, I found that I could speak. Poetry helped me to discover my

own voice and to resurrect my powers of speech. At the same time, poetry led me into the hearts and minds of the poets, giving me a more intimate understanding of the universal human experience. This breakthrough gave me an insatiable appetite for the sheer joy of communicating.

Professor Crouch impressed on me his belief that it would be a tragedy not to store your mind with poems you had memorized, and not to be able to say them out loud. I especially loved Longfellow, Poe, and Shakespeare. I would stand on the stage of the high school auditorium, hold a candle, and recite the poems of Edgar Allan Poe. At home, my Uncle Bob Walker could recite by heart Mark Antony's speech from *Julius Caesar*:

Friends, Romans, countrymen, lend me your ears;
I come to bury Caesar, not to praise him,
The evil that men do lives after them;
The good is oft interred with their bones;
So let it be with Caesar.

In a farm family that considered reading from Shakespeare a fancy pursuit, I was surprised and thrilled to discover that Uncle Bob's joy in the words was contagious. As I worked on our farm in Michigan, I read Shakespeare aloud to myself in the fields. I grew up hearing the great poetry of the King James translation of the Bible, never dreaming that, as an adult, I would be asked to use my voice to record every word of the New Testament.

Just as the troubadour poets sang their words down through the centuries, you, too, can read poetry aloud. Your "podium" may be the stage, the classroom, the living room, the out-of-doors. You may read poems in company or in solitude. You can bring history to life, resurrecting the trials and triumphs of the human spirit.

When asked for advice on reading and writing poetry, the poet Carl Sandburg responded, "Beware of advice, even this." I do not try to give other readers of poetry advice about this highly personal experience—only that they take joy in the words. In this "burst of verses," you will find fun and sorrow, stories and songs, whimsy and majesty. I simply encourage you to enjoy this book, richly stocked with poems about love and pain and danger and hope; about vision and alienation; about art and poetry and life itself.

Whether you "shout them into the teeth of a strong

wind" or whisper them, "down the/river valley on a late summer afternoon," I hope that you will find your own voice and your own pleasure in these poems—and the countless others they will lead you to discover.

POETRY OUT LOUD

The first poems I knew were nursery rhymes, and before I could read them for myself I had come to love just the words of them; the words alone. What the words stood for, symbolised, or meant, was of very secondary importance. What mattered was the sound of them as I heard them for the first time on the lips of the remote and incomprehensible grownups who seemed, for some reason, to be living in my world.

—Dylan Thomas, "Notes on the Art of Poetry"

We begin with the poems and songs of childhood, and we never really leave them behind. Then, in high school and college, they stop being just rhymes to read out loud. They become texts to study, puzzles to solve, enigmas to penetrate. The music goes away, and the complaining starts.

We've heard all the complaints. Poetry these days is too hard or obscure. Too many small editions of undistinguished poems are out there for anyone to keep up with. Poetry speaks a private language that only other poets understand. There's no way for anyone other than an expert to tell good poetry from junk. They don't write 'em like they used to. The smart magazines begin to sound like Alexander Pope,

sneering at bad art: "all nature nods" (falls asleep).

Yet many of us miss the music, the sheer delight in the sound of language. And that is the reason behind *Poetry Out Loud*. It's not a poet's book of poems, or a scholar's. It's a collection of poems gathered together by an informed layman who enjoys poetry out loud—who's even found himself, at times, reciting poems in the shower.

We've read of poetry-reading parties where hosts and guests take turns reciting famous poems to one another. Some hosts start their *own* salons, at which poetry reading is a featured activity—an idea that seems to get revived every few years. Whether you take these poems out of the shower and before an audience is up to you. But you do not have to be a poet to enjoy reading poems aloud, or to do it well.

For that matter, some poets would probably be well advised to let others do the reading for them. William Butler Yeats, whose poems read aloud beautifully, was said to declaim his poems, almost as if incanting some occult spell, in a high monotone that many listeners found annoying; Ezra Pound, who spent several winters as Yeats's secretary, recalled this in one of the Pisan Cantos when he evoked the sound of Yeats working out the lines of "The Peacock" in the drafty stone house they shared in 1913, a sound that seemed:

as it were the wind in the chimney

but was in reality Uncle William

downstairs composing

that had made a great Peeeeeeacock

in the proide ov his oiye

had made a great Peeeeeeeacock in the . . .

made a great peacock

in the proide of his oyyee

proide ov his oy-ee

as indeed he had . . .

This collection aims to explode the idea that poetry belongs only to the creative writing programs; to light a fire under the decorously spare, minimalistic chapbooks on the poetry shelf; to detonate the idea that poetry belongs in the seminar room. Instead of pretending that it is a grave presentation of Great Art that Speaks for Itself, or a lecture on eternal verities, this book takes the role of a slightly irreverent tour guide escorting you through a museum housing both masterpieces and kitsch. The marginal notes, and the notes in the back of the book, seek to strip away the façades that have covered many poems. They're meant to show one reader's arguable understanding of what's going on under the surface, or what was in the background, and suggest the

ways in which poems and poets speak to one another. Though it's bad form to do so these days, I've even simplified some spellings in a few of the older poems.

Certain poems come alive when read out loud. They may wait quietly on the printed page, dressed neatly in rhymes and stanzas, sheltering modestly beneath clever titles. But when read aloud they explode with life and color and fervor. Poetry was a way of speaking before it was a way of writing: it was language arranged memorably, given pattern and form so it would not vanish into empty air—so it could be passed along. That's what makes going to a poetry reading so much more fun than struggling through another thin book in which poems swim page to page in a sea of white space, out of sight of land, or any sort of firm footing that a reader might wish for.

Of course, how a poem sounds when read aloud is not the only thing that counts, but many poems gain something when you hear them. And taking the time to learn to read a poem aloud is a good way to discover how it works. Doing so forces you to think of it not as some eternal work of art, to be admired from a distance, but (to borrow a phrase from Ezra Pound) as something a person might actually say.

Poetry is not a different language, it is *our* language— only stretched, purged of certain habits, intensified by care-

ful choice, made memorable by pattern and rhythm. It is language taken away from its familiar business and made to work more slowly, more exactly. You need not be an expert to enjoy it. Certainly, knowing a little about how poems work can help, but the editor's own experience is that once he stopped studying poetry, he began to enjoy reading it.

So here are famous poems, obscure poems, old poems, and new poems, along with some general background and notes to help make the idea of just reading poems less intimidating. Here are poems by both legendary bards and little-known minor poets; here are children's rhymes and literary landmarks; here you will find humorous ditties, serious literature, raps, blues, easy rhymes, and difficult free verse. The poems here have one thing in common: somehow, because of their rhyme or their rhythm, or the images they summon forth, or the arguments they make, they have caught the attention of an editor who has fun reading poetry out loud—for whom these verses are bursting with life and color and fervor—and who hopes you'll take them to heart, commit a few to memory, and maybe even try them out in your own shower.

—Robert Alden Rubin

I.

POEMS OF LOVE AND WRECKAGE

COURTLY COURTING

Most poetry either follows convention, puts a new twist on it, or flies in its face completely. Here are two poems that just have some fun with two ancient forms. Christopher Marlowe tweaks the pastoral tradition, which dates back to the days of ancient Greece, and which enjoyed a vogue in Marlowe's time. Everyone knows Edward Lear's owl and pussy-cat, but they may not know that they draw on the even older folk tradition of the beast fable.

THE PASSIONATE SHEPHERD TO HIS LOVE
Christopher Marlowe

Come live with me and be my love,
And we will all the pleasures prove
That valleys, groves, hills, and fields,
Woods, or steepy mountain yields.

And we will sit upon the rocks,
Seeing the shepherds feed their flocks,
By shallow rivers to whose falls
Melodious birds sings madrigals.

And I will make thee beds of roses
And a thousand fragrant posies,
A cap of flowers, and a kirtle
Embroidered all with leaves of myrtle.

A gown made of the finest wool
Which from our pretty lambs we pull;
Fair lined slippers for the cold,
With buckles of the purest gold

A belt of straw and ivy buds,
With coral clasps and amber studs;
And if these pleasures may thee move,
Come live with me, and be my love.

The shepherd swains shall dance and sing
For thy delight each May morning
If these delights thy mind may move,
Then live with me and be my love.

PASSIONATE SHEPHERDS

A favorite game of Marie Antoinette was having her ladies dress up as shepherdesses. (Later, at the guillotine, she discovered that *real* shepherds, bakers, shopkeepers, and so forth were somewhat less romantic.) Anyway, this pretty well sums up the convention of pastoral poetry: poets at court writing idealized love poems set amid green grass and rolling hills. Think about it, after all: How many shepherds habitually wear gold, coral, and amber?

Prove = test, try, explore.
Madrigals = songs, usually sung in parts, without instrumentation.
Kirtle = a medieval gown.

THE OWL AND THE PUSSY-CAT
Edward Lear

I

The Owl and the Pussy-Cat went to sea
   In a beautiful pea-green boat,
They took some honey, and plenty of money,
   Wrapped up in a five-pound note.
The Owl looked up to the stars above,
   And sang to a small guitar,
"O lovely Pussy! O Pussy, my love,
   What a beautiful Pussy you are,
      You are,
      You are!
   What a beautiful Pussy you are!"

II

Pussy said to the Owl, "You elegant fowl!
   How charmingly sweet you sing!
O let us be married! too long we have tarried
   But what shall we do for a ring?"
They sailed away, for a year and a day,

To the land where the Bong-tree grows;
And there in a wood a Piggy-wig stood,
  With a ring at the end of his nose,
    His nose,
    His nose,
  With a ring at the end of his nose.

III

"Dear Pig, are you willing to sell for one shilling
  Your ring?" Said the Piggy, "I will."
So they took it away, and were married next day
  By the Turkey who lives on the hill.
They dined on mince, and slices of quince,
  Which they ate with a runcible spoon;
And hand in hand, on the edge of the sand,
  They danced by the light of the moon,
    The moon,
    The moon,
  They danced by the light of the moon.

FABULOUS BEASTS

This bouncy poem is written for its sound and rhythm; there are no hidden messages here. If a cynical modern reader can overlook certain words that have acquired other meanings in recent years, the childlike delight in the improbable, delicious sound of language still shines through.

Runcible spoon = Lear invented this word, which has since come to mean an hors d'oeuvre fork.

BLAZONS TO BEAUTY

Another convention poets keep returning to is the blazon—a descriptive catalog of beauties, usually of the poet's beloved. Here, two of the greatest sonneteers, Spenser and Shakespeare, sing blazons to beauty—one in earnest, one with tongue slightly in cheek.

Both the Indias = the spice-producing East Indies and the gold-rich West Indies.
Spoil = take, plunder.
Sound = free from defects, enduring.
Ween = "beautiful"; Spenser loved old words, and this is an archaic usage derived from Old Norse.

YE TRADEFUL MERCHANTS THAT WITH WEARY TOIL
Edmund Spenser

Ye tradeful Merchants, that with weary toil
Do seek most precious things to make your gain,
And both the Indias of their treasures spoil,
What needeth you to seek so far in vain?
For lo my love doth in her self contain
All this world's riches that may far be found
If Sapphires, lo her eyes be sapphires plain;
If Rubies, lo her lips be rubies sound;
If Pearls, her teeth be pearls both pure and round;
If Ivory, her forehead ivory ween;
If Gold, her locks are finest gold on ground;
If Silver, her fair hands are silver sheen.
But that which fairest is but few behold,
Her mind adorned with virtues manifold.

MY MISTRESS' EYES ARE NOTHING LIKE THE SUN
William Shakespeare

My mistress' eyes are nothing like the sun;
Coral is far more red than her lips' red;
If snow be white, why then her breasts are dun;
If hairs be wires, black wires grow on her head.
I have seen roses damask'd, red and white,
But no such roses see I in her cheeks;
And in some perfumes is there more delight
Than in the breath that from my mistress reeks.
I love to hear her speak, yet well I know
That music hath a far more pleasing sound.
I grant I never saw a goddess go;
My mistress, when she walks, treads on the ground.
    And yet, by heaven, I think my love as rare
    As any she belied with false compare.

The sonnet has become probably the most enduringly popular form for poems in English since it was introduced from Italy and became all the rage in the mid-1500s. Spenser's poem is from his sequence of eighty-one sonnets entitled *Amoretti* ("little love songs").

THE REVERSE BLAZON

Notice how Shakespeare's sonnet turns conventional comparisons on their heads; her lips are pale, not red; hair is conventionally compared to gold wire (hers is black). His mistress is earthy and real, not idealized. By saying what she isn't, the poet says what she is.

Damask'd = red (passion) and white (purity) were combined in the pink damask rose.
Reeks = exhales, emanates; in Shakespeare's day the word did not imply a foul smell.

SKELTONICS

John Skelton was probably the first poet after Chaucer to invent an effective new way of writing English poetry: skeltonic, or "tumbling" verse. It's a bouncy, irreverent, even bawdy poetry that rhymes in unpredictable ways, but one that didn't turn out to be of much use for love songs, or serious poetry. You can see here, and in Ogden Nash's delightful poem about his daughter five hundred years later, how it's perfect for certain light, funny subjects.

Do mi nus / Levavi oculos meos in montes = "The Lord . . . [shall preserve you from all evil]" / "I lift up my eyes to the hills," both drawn from Psalm 121.

FROM PHILIP SPARROW
John Skelton

*D*o mi nus,

Help now, sweet Jesus!

Levavi oculos meos in montes:

Would God I had Zenophontes,

Or Socrates the wise,

To shew me their devise

Moderately to take

This sorrow that I make

For Philip Sparrow's sake!

So fervently I shake,

I feel my body quake;

So urgently I am brought

Into careful thought.

Like Andromaca, Hector's wife,

Was weary of her life,

When she had lost her joy,

Noble Hector of Troy;

In like manner also

Encreaseth my deadly wo,

For my sparrow is go.

It was so pretty a fool,
It would sit on a stool,
And learned after my school
For to keep his cut,
With "Philip, keep your cut!"

It had a velvet cap,
And would sit upon my lap,
And seek after small worms,
And sometime white bread-crumbs;
And many times and oft
Between my breasts soft
It would lie and rest;
It was proper and prest.

Sometime he would gasp
When he saw a wasp;
A fly or a gnat,
He would fly at that;
And pretely he would pant
When he saw an ant.
Lord, how he would pry
After the butterfly!
Lord, how he would hop

STIRRED BY A BIRD

Skeltonics are best read fast, which makes them hardly ideal for an enduring tribute to lost love. Here Skelton imagines a young nun, Jane Scroop, singing a last tribute to her pet sparrow, recently dispatched by a cat. Like conventional poems of love and praise, it calls up classical references and heroic images to praise the dearly departed, which the bouncy verse undercuts. Young Jane, of course, is unaware that sparrows were supposed to be lecherous birds.

Zenophontes = Xenophon, Greek biographer of Socrates.
Devise = guidance, advice.
Andromaca = a model of devotion in the *Iliad*.
Go = departed, gone.
Keep his cut = behave himself.
Cap = markings.
Prest = active.
Gasp = gape.
Pretely = prettily.

Gressop = grasshopper.
Slo = slay.
Fro = from.
Si in i qua ta tes = "If you, Lord, were to note what is done amiss."
De pro fun dis cla ma vi = "Out of the depths have I called . . . [to you , O Lord]," from Psalm 130.

After the gressop!

And whan I said, "Phip, Phip!"

Then he would leap and skip,

And take me by the lip.

Alas, it will me slo,

That Philip is gone me fro!

Si in i qui ta tes,

Alas, I was evil at ease!

De pro fun dis cla ma vi,

When I saw my sparrow die!

THE SNIFFLE
Ogden Nash

In spite of her sniffle,
Isabel's chiffle.
Some girls with a sniffle
Would be weepy and tiffle;
They would look awful,
Like a rained-on waffle,
But Isabel's chiffle
In spite of her sniffle.
Her nose is more red
With a cold in her head,
But then, to be sure,
Her eyes are bluer.
Some girls with a snuffle,
Their tempers are uffle,
But when Isabel's snivelly
She's snivelly civilly,
And when she is snuffly
She's perfectly luffly.

ISABEL'S ILLS

Ogden Nash, whose humorous poems were a regular feature of *The New Yorker* for years, never pretended to write immortal verse; this is supposed to be funny and whimsical, so the bouncy skeltonics work here. Part of what makes this poem come to life is the way Nash takes words that are sometimes pronounced differently than they're spelled and spells them the way they sound. Don't read this as fast as you would a true skeltonic poem, and pause after the really bad rhymes—to let them sink in.

Chiffle = cheerful.
Tiffle = tearful.
Uffle = awful.
Luffly = lovely.

BEFORE BEDTIME, AND AFTER

The poet, the saying goes, always gets the girl. The seductive logic of Andrew Marvell's famous poem should confirm that it's nothing new. Here is the poet as Bad Boy. He puts a suggestive spin on a theme from classical Roman poetry, inviting his love to "seize the day" (*carpe diem*), among other things. Nikki Giovanni, showing us the other side of the coin, sings a modern-day blues—the song of a woman who's seized the day a few times too often and is starting to wonder if there's anything else to hold on to.

Ganges / Humber = rivers on opposite sides of the world.
Complain = write poems about unrequited love.

TO HIS COY MISTRESS
Andrew Marvell

Had we but world enough, and time,

This coyness, Lady, were no crime.

We would sit down, and think which way

To walk, and pass our long love's day.

Thou by the Indian Ganges' side

Shouldst rubies find; I by the tide

Of Humber would complain. I would

Love you ten years before the flood,

And you should, if you please, refuse

Till the Conversion of the Jews.

My vegetable love should grow

Vaster than empires and more slow;

An hundred years should go to praise

Thine eyes, and on thy forehead gaze;

Two hundred to adore each breast,

But thirty thousand to the rest;

An age at least to every part,

And the last age should show your heart.

For, Lady, you deserve this state,

Nor would I love at lower rate.

But at my back I always hear
Time's wingèd chariot hurrying near;
And yonder all before us lie
Deserts of vast eternity.
Thy beauty shall no more be found,
Nor, in thy marble vault, shall sound
My echoing song; then worms shall try
That long-preserved virginity,
And your quaint honor turns to dust,
And into ashes all my lust
The grave's a fine and private place,
But none, I think, do there embrace.

Now therefore, while the youthful hue
Sits on thy skin like morning dew,
And while thy willing soul transpires
At every pore with instant fires,
Now let us sport us while we may,
And now, like amorous birds of prey,
Rather at once our time devour
Than languish in his slow-chapt power.
Let us roll all our strength and all
Our sweetness up into one ball,
And tear our pleasures with rough strife

MY VEGETABLE LOVE
One function of classical poetry was arguing ideas logically. Marvell makes a relentlessly logical three part argument about love: (1) if we had plenty of time, you could flirt as long as you wanted; (2) but we're getting old; (3) so come live with me and be my love. Notice how blazons to beauty become part of the argument. Marvell's poem is like a singles' bar seduction—full of raised eyebrows and double entendres. The poet makes the object of his affections feel beautiful and sexy, then proceeds to prove why he should be the lucky guy.

Before the flood / Conversion of the Jews = from before Noah to the last Judgment.
Vegetable love = slow-growing, deep-rooted.
Quaint honor = a lewd pun on virginity, based on the archaic word *queynte*.
Sport us = enjoy ourselves.

Thorough the iron gates of life;
Thus, though we cannot make our sun
Stand still, yet we will make him run.

MASTER CHARGE BLUES
Nikki Giovanni

it's wednesday night baby
and i'm all alone
wednesday night baby
and i'm all alone
sitting with myself
waiting for the telephone

wanted you baby
but you said you had to go
wanted you yeah
but you said you had to go
called your best friend
but he can't come 'cross no more

did you ever go to bed
at the end of a busy day
look over and see the smooth
where your hump usta lay
feminine odor and no reason why
i said feminine odor and no reason why
asked the lord to help me
he shook his head "not i"

but i'm a modern woman baby
ain't gonna let this get me down
i'm a modern woman
ain't gonna let this get me down
gonna take my master charge
and get everything in town

SEIZE THE MORNING AFTER

Carpe deim isn't all it's
cracked up to be (ain't
nothing but the blues).
Imagine a blues harmonica
playing behind you as you
recite this poem. After
every two lines, it chimes
in "da-DA da-dum." A blues
song traditionally repeats
its first line twice, and then
pauses halfway through the
third line. Poets call this
pause a *caesura*. (Blues
singers probably call it a
pause.) To see how Nikki
Giovanni's poem does this
in the first stanza, read
lines 1 and 2 as one line,
lines 3 and 4 as one line,
and pause between lines 5
and 6.

DANCING THE NIGHT AWAY

Here are two more Bad Boys. Their poems share an attitude in which the woman is idealized, but (as with Marvell's "To His Coy Mistress") carnal thoughts are part of the tribute. Ernest Dowson belonged to The Rhymer's Club, a group of late-nineteenth-century poets who (according to the group's most famous member, W. B. Yeats) spent much of the time drugged or drunk on absinthe, writing poems to ethereal beauty. Theodore Roethke was a troubled alcoholic as well, though his poem, full of outrageous puns and allusions, is more playful and less anguished.

NON SUM QUALIS ERAM BONAE SUB REGNO CYNARAE
Ernest Dowson

Last night, ah, yesternight, betwixt her lips and mine
There fell thy shadow, Cynara! thy breath was shed
Upon my soul between the kisses and the wine;
And I was desolate and sick of an old passion,
    Yea, I was desolate and bowed my head:
I have been faithful to thee, Cynara! in my fashion.

All night upon mine heart I felt her warm heart beat,
Night-long within mine arms in love and sleep she lay;
Surely the kisses of her bought red mouth were sweet;
But I was desolate and sick of an old passion,
    When I awoke and found the dawn was gray:
I have been faithful to thee, Cynara! in my fashion.

I have forgot much, Cynara! gone with the wind,
flung roses, roses riotously with the throng,
Dancing, to put thy pale, lost lilies out of mind;
But I was desolate and sick of an old passion,
    Yea, all the time, because the dance was long:
I have been faithful to thee, Cynara! in my fashion.

I cried for madder music and for stronger wine,
But when the feast is finished and the lamps expire,
Then falls thy shadow, Cynara! the night is thine;
And I am desolate and sick of an old passion,
    Yea, hungry for the lips of my desire:
I have been faithful to thee, Cynara! in my fashion.

BITTER TASTES

The rhymes here are repetitive—the rhyme of *passion* and *fashion* repeats four times in a refrain; *wine/wind/wine* rhyme with *wine/mind/thine*. The repetition gives the poem a driven intensity, a quality also apparent in *villanelles* such as those by Thomas, Bishop, and Empson, elsewhere in this book.

Non Sum Qualis eram Bonae sub Regno Cynarae = "I am not what I was under the rule of the kind Cynara." Don't be put off by the Latin, which is from an ode by Horace and mostly seems meant to give the poem some gravity. The name Cynara is associated with bitterness; it's also the botanical name for the artichoke, for whatever that's worth.
Bought = she's a prostitute.

Traditional blazons (written by English poets who grew up reading Greek) sometimes praised the beloved's interior beauty. Here Roethke delights in that idea, praising her bones, and the way they move under her skin. In fact, there are so many plays on words and convention going on in this extended blazon that it's pointless to try to catalog all the puns or explain them to your listeners. Some will get them—most won't. Some of the rhymes (*bones/one*) (*them/contain*) are partial, and only become apparent on paper. Don't try to stress them when reading aloud.

I KNEW A WOMAN
Theodore Roethke

I knew a woman, lovely in her bones,
When small birds sighed, she would sigh back at them;
Ah, when she moved, she moved more ways than one:
The shapes a bright container can contain!
Of her choice virtues only gods should speak,
Or English poets who grew up on Greek
(I'd have them sing in chorus, cheek to cheek).

How well her wishes went! She stroked my chin,
She taught me Turn, and Counter-turn, and Stand;
She taught me Touch, that undulant white skin;
I nibbled meekly from her proffered hand;
She was the sickle; I, poor I, the rake,
Coming behind her for her pretty sake
(But what prodigious mowing we did make).

Love likes a gander, and adores a goose:
Her full lips pursed, the errant note to seize;
She played it quick, she played it light and loose;
My eyes, they dazzled at her flowing knees;
Her several parts could keep a pure repose,
Or one hip quiver with a mobile nose
(She moved in circles, and those circles moved).

Let seed be grass, and grass turn into hay:
I'm martyr to a motion not my own;
What's freedom for? To know eternity.
I swear she cast a shadow white as stone.
But who would count eternity in days?
These old bones live to learn her wanton ways:
(I measure time by how a body sways).

Turn, Counter-turn, Stand =
a Greek *ode* traditionally
was sung by a chorus in a
kind of three-part dance—
the *strophe* (or "turn")
was sung walking one
direction, the antistrophe
(or "counter-turn") was
sung walking the opposite
direction, and the *epode*
(or "stand") was sung
standing still.
Rake = this pun on rake-
hell, or ladies' man, gives
this passage a naughty turn.
Nose = a taster's term for
the aroma of wine.

MORNING AND EVENING

These two are hard. One of John Donne's favorite devices was to imagine a little world with everything in it, a microcosm.

Here, the poet, who is initially grumpy at being awakened by the sun that shines in on him and his lover, and then pleased because he can see her in the sunlight, begins to entertain the idea that the whole world—vast and newly discovered—can be found in their room. Amy Clampitt, watching the sun set in a different time and place, wonders what Donne would think of it, and notes sadly that she cannot see things the way he did, four centuries and half a world away.

THE SUN RISING
John Donne

Busy old fool, unruly sun,
  Why dost thou thus,
Through windows, and through curtains call on us?
Must to thy motions lovers' seasons run?
    Saucy pedantic wretch, go chide
    Late schoolboys and sour prentices,
  Go tell court-huntsmen that the king will ride,
  Call country ants to harvest offices;
Love, all alike, no season knows, nor clime,
Nor hours, days, months, which are the rags of time.

    Thy beams, so reverend, and strong
      Why shouldst thou think?
  I could eclipse and cloud them with a wink,
  But that I would not lose her sight so long:
      If her eyes have not blinded thine,
      Look, and tomorrow late, tell me,
  Whether both the' Indias of spice and mine
  Be where thou left'st them, or lie here with me.

Ask for those kings whom thou saw'st yesterday,
And thou shalt hear, All here in one bed lay.

    She'is all states, and all princes, I;
      Nothing else is.
   Princes do but play us; compar'd to this,
   All honor's mimic, all wealth alchemy.
    Thou, sun, art half as happy'as we,
     In that the world's contracted thus;
  Thine age asks ease, and since thy duties be
  To warm the world, that's done in warming us.
Shine here to us, and thou art everywhere;
This bed thy center is, these walls, thy sphere.

SASSING THE SUN

Conventional love poets praised old Sol, but here the poet insults him.

Pedantic = the sun insists on punctuality.
Prentices = apprentices.
Harvest offices = agricultural tasks.
Both the'India's of spice and mine = see "To His Coy Mistress."
Mimic = pretense; mimicry.
Alchemy = alchemists claimed to turn lead to gold, but were charlatans.

Printers and poets often used apostrophes to show when a syllable shouldn't be pronounced. Donne does this several times: *the'Indias* (pronounced "thindias"), *she'is* (pronouced "she's"), *happy'as* (pronounced "hap yas"); but notice that *compar'd* is pronounced like the modern "compared."

JOHN DONNE IN CALIFORNIA
Amy Clampitt

THE POET IN THE POEM

Clampitt's poem alludes to
another Donne poem,
"Hymn to God My God, in
My Sickness," in which the
poet ponders death and
imagines the whole world
(particularly the Pacific
Ocean) from his sickbed,
much as he does in "The
Sun Rising." Clampitt,
herself pondering all this
amid the weird plants of
modern-day California, has
a far less comforting, and
more disconcerting, vision
of the world's vastness.

I s the Pacific Sea my home? Or is

Jerusalem? pondered John Donne,

who never stood among these strenuous,

huge, wind-curried hills, their green

gobleted just now with native poppies'

opulent red-gold, where New World lizards run

among strange bells, thistles wear the guise

of lizards, and one shining oak is poison;

or cast an eye on lofted strong-arm

redwoods' fog-fondled silhouette,

their sapling wisps among the ferns in time

more his (perhaps) than our compeer: here at

the round earth's numbly imagined rim,

its ridges drowned in the irradiating vat

of evening, the land ends; the magnesium

glare whose unbridged nakedness is bright

beyond imagining, begins. John Donne,
I think, would have been more at home
than the frail wick of metaphor I've brought
to see by, and cannot, for the conflagration
of this nightfall's utter strangeness.

*More his (perhaps) than
our compeer* = the long-lived
redwood trees were proba-
bly saplings in Donne's day.
Magnesium glare = this
may refer to the blinding
reflection of the setting sun
over the western ocean.
Frail wick of metaphor =
Donne is Clampitt's
metaphor here, and she
finds him inadequate to
explain the strangeness of
what she sees; the real
Donne, she suggests,
would have an easier time
finding poetic images to
explain the disconcerting
feeling she gets as she
watches the sun set.

THAT COME HITHER LOOK

Sir Thomas Wyatt—who wrote his poems a quarter century before Shakespeare was born—is often given a good deal of the credit for introducing the sonnet to English poetry, and for coming up with a rough, vigorous pacing that later writers perfected and turned into regular *iambic pentameter*—which remains the dominant rhythmic line for poetry in English. You can see something of its power in Gerald Barrax's poem, where a single line, borrowed from Wyatt, makes the whole poem reverberate.

THEY FLEE FROM ME THAT SOMETIME DID ME SEEK
Sir Thomas Wyatt

They flee from me that sometime did me seek,
With naked foot stalking in my chamber.
I have seen them gentle, tame, and meek
That now are wild and do not remember
That sometime they put themselves in danger
To take bread at my hand; and now they range
Busily seeking with a continual change.

Thanked be fortune, it hath been otherwise
Twenty times better; but once in special,
In thin array after a pleasant guise,
When her loose gown from her shoulders did fall,
And she me caught in her arms long and small,
Therewithall sweetly did me kiss,
And softly said, "Dear heart, how like you this?"

It was no dream, I lay broad waking.
But all is turned thorough my gentleness,
Into a strange fashion of forsaking;
And I have leave to go of her goodness,
And she also to use newfangleness.
But since that I so kindely am served,
I would fain know what she hath deserved.

OLD NEWFANGLENESS

This poem isn't a sonnet, and it isn't regular, but certain lines show off Wyatt's innovation—combining the strengths of *accentual* verse (which counts the number of stresses in a line) with *syllabic* verse (which counts the total number of syllables) into an English poetic line that had both force and rhythm. *Iambic* describes the rhythmic stress "da-DUM"; *pentameter* means there are five such *iambs*—or ten syllables total. You can see it in the first line, "They FLEE from ME that SOMEtime DID me SEEK."

In special = especially.
Thin array after a pleasant guise = a provocative and pleasing style.
Small = slender.
Thorough = through.
Newfangleness = fickleness.
Kindely = kindly, rightly, politely, as befitting one who is kin (all of these, of course, are meant sarcastically).
Fain = rather.

FOURTH DANCE POEM
Gerald W. Barrax

The White Lady has asked me to dance.
She had been lurking under the bridge I had to cross
    to go anywhere.
I've considered my answer
and since I've stopped denying it
           she knows I have natural rhythm
so will she believe I dont know this dance?

"Why dance we not? Why stand we still?"

She has seen the white feather
I wear in my cap like a plume
and doubts my honesty
but I say to her anyway
ah White Lady
but I dont know this dance.

She hasnt believed me.

"They flee from me that sometime did me seek."

Oh White Lady
now you've said it

for me it was a long walk from Alabama

and I was on my way anywhere

WHITE LADIES
Barrax, an African-
American poet from
Alabama, notes that "in
legend, the appearance of
White Ladies usually fore-
bodes death. In Normandy
they lurk on bridges and
other narrow places and
ask the traveler to dance. If
he refuses the Lady he is
thrown into a ditch."

II.

LIGHT VERSE AND POEMS THAT TELL STORIES

RHYMES WITHOUT REASON

Dr. Seuss made a fortune for himself and his publishers by bringing together two of the things that lend themselves most readily to poetry read aloud—whimsical rhyme and storytelling. Even if you don't have much of a memory for "serious" poetry, you probably remember a verse from *Green Eggs and Ham*. Certain poets specialize in children's rhymes and light verse, but even our greatest poets have delighted in it too, simply because it's so much fun.

There was an Old Lady whose folly,
Induced her to sit in a holly;
Whereon, by a thorn her dress being torn,
She quickly became melancholy.
　　　　—Edward Lear

There was an old man of Calcutta
Who coated his tonsils with butta,
Thus converting his snore
From a thunderous roar
To a soft, oleaginous mutta.
　　　　—Ogden Nash

There was a young curate of Kew,
Who kept a tom cat in a pew;
　　He taught it to speak
　　Alphabetical Greek,
But it never got further than μ.
　　　　—Anonymous

For travelers going sidereal
The danger they say is bacterial.
I don't know the pattern
On Mars or on Saturn
But on Venus it must be venereal.

—Robert Frost

The limerick packs laughs anatomical
Into space that is quite economical,
    But the good ones I've seen
    So seldom are clean,
And the clean ones so seldom are comical.

—Anonymous

LIMERICKS AND CLERIHEWS

Where limericks have strict rules for rhyme and rhythm, and most people know them by heart anyway, the rules for clerihews are less familiar. Limericks were all the craze in the mid-1800s, and circulated the way a good joke does nowadays. Though Edward Lear didn't invent the form, he made it popular. Ogden Nash's limericks were quoted so often that he gave them names. He called the one printed here, "Arthur."

μ = the name for the Greek letter "M" is pronounced "mew."

M arcel Proust

Thought a lot about being seduced,
But as this was too exciting,
He just put it in writing.

—Paul Horgan

William Penn
Was the most level-headed of men;
He had only one mania—
Pennsylvania.

—William Jay Smith

Les Matins dans la Rue fleurus no. 27
Gertrude Stein
arose at nine

and arose and arose and arose
and arose

—Jonathan Williams

Lady Mary Whortley Montagu
Refused to use the accent aigu.
This whim, which her friends thought curious,
Made the French furious.

—Jacques Barzun

The digestion of Milton
Was unequal to Stilton.
He was only feeling so-so
When he wrote Il Penseroso.

— Edmund Clerihew Bentley

Clerihews, named after their inventor, Edmund Clerihew Bentley, have never achieved the wide popularity of limericks. Usually the first line is someone's name, which rhymes with the second line. The third and fourth lines also rhyme. They're harder to do well, a bit more highbrow and genteel—the kind of thing that gets posted on faculty office doors in English departments.

Les Matins dans la Rue fleurus no. 27 = the title of the clerihew means, "Mornings at 27 Rue fleurus" (Gertrude Stein's address in Paris).
Lady Mary Whortley Montagu = English author and wit in the 1800s.
Il Penseroso = John Milton's famous poem on melancholy.

SENSE AND NONSENSE

A *nonsense verse* is like a child playing—there's usually some logic, but it doesn't follow "grown-up" rules. Its inventions and unlikely combinations are its charm. Here, Lewis Carroll invents imaginary words, but the *sense* of English grammar is so strong he can tell a story anyway. E. E. Cummings, on the other hand, uses real words in seemingly ungrammatical and non-sensical ways. What makes Carroll's poem "nonsense" is its lack of any serious message; Cummings's poem, for all its strangeness, has a point to make.

JABBERWOCKY
Lewis Carroll

'Twas brillig, and the slithy toves
    Did gyre and gimble in the wabe;
All mimsy were the borogoves,
    And the mome raths outgrabe.

"Beware the Jabberwock, my son!
    The jaws that bite, the claws that catch!
Beware the Jubjub bird, and shun
    The frumious Bandersnatch!"

He took his vorpal sword in hand:
    Long time the manxome foe he sought—
So rested he by the Tumtum tree,
    And stood awhile in thought.

And as in uffish thought he stood,
    The Jabberwock, with eyes of flame,
Came whiffling through the tulgey wood,
    And burbled as it came!

One, two! One, two! And through and through
  The vorpal blade went snicker-snack!
He left it dead, and with its head
  He went galumphing back.

"And hast thou slain the Jabberwock?
  Come to my arms, my beamish boy!
O frabjous day! Callooh! Callay!"
  He chortled in his joy.

'Twas brillig, and the slithy toves
  Did gyre and gimble in the wabe
All mimsy were the borogoves,
  And the mome raths outgrabe.

THROUGH THE LOOKING-GLASS
Alice happens on this poem in the land on the other side of the mirror in *Alice through the Looking-Glass*. To read it, she must hold it up to a mirror. Later, Humpty-Dumpty explains what some of the nonsense words mean, but it would spoil the fun to do so here. It's worth noting that *chortle*, which Humpty Dumpty says is a blend of *chuckle* and *snort*, can now be found in standard dictionaries.

"Jabberwocky" is squarely in the tradition of the story-telling poem, or ballad. Read it the way you would a "Once upon a time" fairy tale—the more sound effects, the better.

ANYONE LIVED IN A PRETTY HOW TOWN
E. E. Cummings

anyone lived in a pretty how town
(with up so floating many bells down)
spring summer autumn winter
he sang his didn't he danced his did.

Women and men(both little and small)
cared for anyone not at all
they sowed their isn't they reaped their same
sun moon stars rain

children guessed(but only a few
and down they forgot as up they grew
autumn winter spring summer)
that noone loved him more by more

when by now and tree by leaf
she laughed his joy she cried his grief
bird by snow and stir by still
anyone's any was all to her

someones married their everyones
laughed their cryings and did their dance
(sleep wake hope and then)they
said their nevers they slept their dream

stars rain sun moon
(and only the snow can begin to explain
how children are apt to forget to remember
with up so floating many bells down)

one day anyone died i guess
(and noone stooped to kiss his face)
busy folk buried them side by side
little by little and was by was

all by all and deep by deep
and more by more they dream their sleep
noone and anyone earth by april
wish by spirit and if by yes.

Women and men(both dong and ding)
summer autumn winter spring
reaped their sowing and went their came
sun moon stars rain

Like "Jabberwocky," this is a storytelling poem, with strong rhymes, that should be read much as you would a fairy tale. It's the story of two lovers, *anyone* and *noone*—a sweet tale of two small people who find each other and whom the world, fortunately, fails to notice. Cummings rebelled against the rules of punctuation (even refusing to capitalize his own name, signing it *e. e. cummings*). Don't be put off by it, or by his displacements of words. A "little how town" might mean, for example, a little town where people ask "how?" dumbly, without a clue that a wider world exists beyond the town limits. It's a puzzle for you to figure out.

STORYTELLING

The great stories of classical and medieval times—Homer's *Iliad* and *Odyssey*, Virgil's *Aeneid*, the anonymously authored *Beowulf*, Chaucer's *Canterbury Tales*, and so forth—were all verse. In recent times, though a few poets carry on the tradition of long narrative poems, verse storytelling has pretty much been relegated to satire and light verse, such as Ernest Lawrence Thayer's famous "Casey at the Bat." In the 1980s and 1990s rap music—as in the next poem, Slick Rick's "Children's Story" —has brought back popular storytelling in which rhythmic speech, not melody, takes center stage.

CASEY AT THE BAT
Ernest Lawrence Thayer

It looked extremely rocky for the Mudville nine that day;
The score stood two to four with but one inning left to play.
So, when Cooney died at second, and Burrows did the same,
A pallor wreathed the features of the patrons of the game.

A straggling few got up to go, leaving there the rest,
With that hope which springs eternal within the human breast.
For they thought: "If only Casey could get a whack at that,"
They'd put even money now, with Casey at the bat.

But Flynn preceded Casey, and likewise so did Blake,
And the former was a pudd'n and the latter was a fake.
So on that stricken multitude a death-like silence sat;
For there seemed but little chance of Casey's getting to the bat.

But Flynn let drive a "single," to the wonderment of all.
And the much despisèd Blakey "tore the cover off the ball."
And when the dust had lifted, and they saw what had
        occurred,
There was Blakey safe on second, and Flynn a-huggin' third.

Then from the gladdened multitude went up a joyous yell—
It bounded from the mountaintops, it rattled in the dell;
It struck upon the hillside and rebounded on the flat;
For Casey, mighty Casey, was advancing to the bat.

There was ease in Casey's manner as he stepped into his place,
There was pride in Casey's bearing and a smile on Casey's face;
And when responding to the cheers he lightly doffed his hat,
No stranger in the crowd could doubt, 'twas Casey at the bat.

Ten thousand eyes were on him as he rubbed his hands
    with dirt,
five thousand tongues applauded when he wiped them on
    his shirt;
Then when the writhing pitcher ground the ball into his hip,
Defiance glanced in Casey's eye, a sneer curled Casey's lip.

And now the leather-covered sphere came hurtling through
    the air,
And Casey stood a-watching it in haughty grandeur there;
Close by the sturdy batsman the ball unheeded sped;
"That hain't my style," said Casey. "Strike one," the umpire said.

HUBRIS AT HOME PLATE

If you can imagine it, one of the great translations of the *Iliad* is in a form similar to the one Thayer uses—*fourteeners* (a seven-beat iambic line). It was a slow, clunky, awkward form for heroic poetry. The long lines of "Casey" are slightly different—most of them pause slightly midway through, so they sound more like a traditional ballad—but the long lines also give a mock gravity to the Casey tragedy.

"Casey" first appeared in a San Francisco newspaper and was soon wildly popular across the United States. Part of its appeal is that baseball becomes the setting for a mock-heroic tragedy. Tragedy, as defined by the ancient Greeks, was the fall of a great man, brought about by *hubris*—arrogance, or excessive pride. Many of those same elements are described in Thayer's poem, but with tongue firmly in cheek.

From the benches, black with people, there went up a muffled
    roar,
Like the beating of the storm waves on a stern and distant
    shore.
"Kill him! kill the umpire!" shouted someone from the stand;
And it's likely they'd have killed him had not Casey raised his
    hand.

With a smile of Christian charity great Casey's visage shone;
He stilled the rising tumult , he made the game go on;
He signalled to the pitcher, and once more the spheroid flew;
But Casey still ignored it, and the umpire said, "Strike two."

"Fraud!" cried the maddened thousands, and the echo
    answered, "Fraud!"
But one scornful look from Casey and the audience was awed;
They saw his face grow stern and cold, they saw his muscles
    strain,
And they knew that Casey wouldn't let the ball go by again.

The sneer is gone from Casey's lips, his teeth are clenched
    in hate,
He pounds with cruel vengeance his bat upon the plate;
And now the pitcher holds the ball, and now he lets it go,
And now the air is shattered by the force of Casey's blow.

Oh, somewhere in this favored land the sun is shining bright,

The band is playing somewhere, and somewhere hearts are
   light;

And somewhere men are laughing, and somewhere children
   shout,

But there is no joy in Mudville—Mighty Casey has struck out.

CHILDREN'S STORY
Ricky Walters

Once upon a time not long ago

When people wore pajamas and lived life slow

When laws were stern and justice stood

And people were behavin' like they ought to: good

There lived a little boy who was misled

By another little boy and this is what he said:

"Me and you, Ty, we're gonna make some cash

Robbin' old folks and making the dash"

They did the job, money came with ease

But one couldn't stop. It's like he had a disease

He robbed another and another and a sister and her
   brother

Tried to rob a man who was a Dt. undercover

ONCE UPON A TIME
Will things come full circle? Are there rap epics in the future? Some literary scholars now think that ancient Anglo-Saxon poetry was meant to be recited along with the rhythmic accompaniment of a musical instrument. That was certainly true of ancient Greek poetry, recited to the strummings of the traditional poet's harp, or lyre (from which we get "lyrics"). Rap's popularity owes as much to "krush grooves" and dance beats as to its lyrics, but the rhythmic, rhyming *message* of many raps is what gives them their power. Though its meter is rough and changeable, Slick Rick's bouncy, streetwise lyric basically maintains a four-beat accentual line. It should be read fast, even breathlessly, with anger and irony.

The cop grabbed his arm, he started acting erratic
He said, "Keep still, boy, no need for static"
Punched him in his belly and he gave him a slap
But little did he know the little boy was strapped
The kid pulled out a gun. He said, "Why'd you hit me?"
The barrel was set straight for the cop's kidney
The cop got scared. The kid, he starts to figure:
"I'll get years if I pull this trigger."
So he cold dashed and ran around the block
Cop radios in to another lady cop
He ran by a tree, there he saw this sister.
Shot for the head. He shot back and missed her
Looked 'round good and from expectations
He decided he'd head for the subway stations
But she was comin' and he made a left
He was runnin' top speed till he was out of breath
Knocked an old man down and swore he killed 'im
Then he made his move to an abandoned buildin'
Ran up the stairs, up to the top floor
Opened up a door there. Guess who he saw?
Dave, the dope fiend, shootin' dope
Who don't know the meanin' of water nor soap
He said, "I need bullets! Hurry up! Run!"

The dope fiend brought back a spankin' shotgun
He went outside but there was cops all over
Then he dipped into a car, a stolen Nova
Raced up the block doin' eighty-three
Crashed into a tree near University
Escaped alive, though the car was battered
Rat-a-tat-tatted and all the cops scattered
Ran out of bullets and he still had static
Grabbed a pregnant lady and pulled out the automatic
Pointed at her head, he said the gun was full of lead
He told the cops, "Back off, or honey here's dead!"
Deep in his heart he knew he was wrong
So he let the lady go and he starts to run on
Sirens sounded, he seemed astounded
And before long the little boy got surrounded
He dropped the gun. So went the glory
And this is the way I must end this story:
He was only seventeen, in a madman's dream
The cops shot the kid. I still hear him scream
This ain't funny, so don't you dare laugh
Just another case about the wrong path
Straight and narrow, or your soul gets cast
Good night!

CAMP SONGS

Rudyard Kipling was tremendously popular as the voice of the untutored Imperial British foot soldier around the turn of the century. We can see the seductive rhythm of his lyrics, also the condescension and bigoted sentiment that make them dated today. "Let little kiplings rant," Australian aboriginal poet Kath Walker wrote in one of her poems, "White People." Walker seeks to convey and celebrate the traditional preliterate culture that Kipling's generation and its predecessors mostly obliterated—a culture vanishing as Australia modernizes—without overromanticizing it.

Fuzzy Wuzzy
Rudyard Kipling
(Sudan Expeditionary Force)

We've fought with many men acrost the seas,
  An' some of 'em was brave an' some was not:
The Paythan an' the Zulu an' Burmese;
  But the Fuzzy was the finest o' the lot.
We never got a ha'porth's change of 'im:
  'E squatted in the scrub an' 'ocked our 'orses,
'E cut our sentries up at *Suakim*,
  An' 'e played the cat an' banjo with our forces.
    So 'ere's *to* you, Fuzzy-Wuzzy, at your 'ome in the
      Sowdan;
    You're a pore benighted 'eathen but a first-class
      fightin' man;
    We gives you your certifikit, an' if you want it
      signed
    We'll come an' 'ave a romp with you whenever
      you're inclined.

We took our chanst among the Kyber 'ills,
  The Boers knocked us silly at a mile,
The Burman guv us Irriwaddy chills,

An' a Zulu *impi* dished us up in style:

But all we ever got from such as they

    Was pop to what the Fuzzy made us swaller;

We 'eld our bloomin' own, the papers say,

    But man for man the Fuzzy knocked us 'oller.

        Then 'ere's *to* you, Fuzzy-Wuzzy, an' the missis
           and the kid;

        Our orders was to break you, an' of course we
           went an' did.

        We sloshed you with Martinis, an' it wasn't 'ardly
           fair;

        But for all the odds agin you, Fuzzy-Wuz, you bruk
           the square.

'E 'asn't got no papers of 'is own,

    'E 'asn't got no medals nor rewards,

So we must certify the skill 'e's shown

    In usin' of 'is long two-'anded swords:

When 'e's 'oppin' in an' out among the bush

    With 'is coffin-'eaded shield an' shovel-spear,

A 'appy day with Fuzzy on the rush

    Will last a 'ealthy Tommy for a year.

    So 'ere's *to* you, Fuzzy-Wuzzy, an' your friends

    which is no more,

WHEN THE SUN NEVER SET

Kipling imitates the lower-class accent of British footsoldiers by dropping consonants and changing spellings, which makes it hard to recite today without practice. Try to adopt the rough, condescending attitude of the speaker when you read it. At the time, the army was constantly called on to put down rebellions throughout Asia and Africa. In 1881, the Sudanese led by Muhammad Ahmed, the *Mahdi* (Messiah), revolted against British and Egyptian rule; the revolt was not put down until 1898. At the battle of Tamai, 1883, the famed British "hollow square," a defensive formation in use since Waterloo, was broken for the first time in military history.

If we 'adn't lost some messmates we would 'elp
    you to deplore;
But give an' take's the gospel, an' we'll call the
    bargain fair,
For if you 'ave lost more than us, you crumpled up
    the square!

'E rushes at the smoke when we let drive,
    An', before we know, 'e's 'ackin' at our 'ead;
'E's all 'ot sand an' ginger when alive,
    An' 'e's generally shammin' when 'e's dead.
'E's a daisy, 'e's a ducky, 'e's a lamb!
    'E's a injia-rubber idiot on the spree,
'E's the on'y thing that doesn't care a damn
    For the Regiment o' British Infantree.
        So 'ere's *to* you, Fuzzy-Wuzzy, at your 'ome in the
            Sowdan;
        You're a pore benighted 'eathen but a first-class
            fightin' man;
        And 'ere's *to* you, Fuzzy-Wuzzy, with your 'ayrick
            'ead of 'air—
        You big black boundin' beggar—for you bruk a
            British square.

CORROBOREE
Kath Walker

Hot day dies, cook time comes.
Now between the sunset and the sleep-time
Time of playabout.
The hunters paint black bodies by firelight with designs of
meaning
To dance corroboree.
Now didgeridoo compels with haunting drone eager feet
    to stamp,
Click sticks click in rhythms to swaying bodies
Dancing corroboree.
Like spirit things from the great surrounding dark
Ghost-gums dimly seen stand at the edge of light
Watching corroboree.
Eerie the scene in leaping firelight,
Eerie the sounds in that wild setting,
As naked dancers weave stories of the tribe
Into corroboree.

FIRELIGHT DANCING

Kath Walker's poem evokes the sense of the traditional dance rather than the foreign rhythms of English poetry. Notice how the sounds and rhythms of certain lines are repeated. Walker's books are full of protest, but they also seek to explain aboriginal culture to a mostly white audience. Here, she evokes a traditional dance with instruments and symbols that belong to a vanishing culture.

Didgeridoo = a large hollow pipe that produces a droning, buzzing music.

VOICES FROM BEYOND

The traditional storytelling poem is the ballad. No one quite knows when a poem such as "The Unquiet Grave" was first composed, only that it was memorized, passed down, and improved on by succeeding generations until someone finally wrote it down. At the core of most ballads is an ancient folk tradition— in this case, the idea that excessive grief disturbs the dead. Edwin Arlington Robinson takes a similar notion but frames it in social and personal terms—as a piece of the past that must be forgotten if he is to carry on with the business of life.

THE UNQUIET GRAVE
Traditional British ballad

"The wind doth blow today, my love,
    And a few small drops of rain;
I never had but one true-love,
    In cold grave she was lain.

"I'll do as much for my true-love
    As any young man may;
I'll sit and mourn all at her grave
    For a twelvemonth and a day."

The twelvemonth and a day being up
    The dead began to speak
"Oh who sits weeping on my grave
    And will not let me sleep?"

"'Tis I my love sits on your grave
    And will not let you sleep;
For I crave one kiss of your clay-cold lips
    And that is all I seek."

"You crave one kiss of my clay-cold lips;
　　But my breath smells earthy strong;
If you have one kiss of my clay-cold lips
　　Your time will not be long.

"'Tis down in yonder garden green
　　Love where we used to walk
The finest flower that ere was seen
　　Is withered to a stalk.

"The stalk is withered dry, my love,
　　So will our hearts decay;
So make yourself content, my love,
　　Till God calls you away."

LOATHLY LADY

Ballad meter is easy and familiar, with a four-beat line followed by a three-beat line. Many traditional ballads have been set to music. This one lacks the refrain, or repeated verse, that is common in many other ballads. Besides being a good advertisement for mouthwash, "The Unquiet Grave" echoes another traditional folk theme (though only slightly) —that of the "loathly lady," a hag or ugly woman who must be kissed by the hero. Some scholars have suggested that it actually may be newer than most traditional ballads—possibly written as late as the 1800s.

CALVERLY'S
Edwin Arlington Robinson

We go no more to Calverly's
For there the lights are few and low;
And who are there to see by them,
Or what they see, we do not know.
Poor strangers of another tongue
May now creep in from anywhere,
And we, forgotten, be no more
Than twilight on a ruin there.

We two, the remnant. All the rest
Are cold and quiet. You nor I,
Nor fiddle now, nor flagon-lid,
May ring them back from where they lie.
No fame delays oblivion
For them, but something yet survives:
A record written fair, could we
But read the book of scattered lives.

There'll be a page for Leffingwell,
And one for Lingard, the Moon-calf;
And who knows what for Clavering,
Who died because he couldn't laugh?
Who knows or cares? No sign is here,
No face, no voice, no memory;
No Lingard with his eerie joy,
No Clavering, no Calverly.

We cannot have them here with us
To say where their light lives are gone,
Or if they be of other stuff
Than are the moons of Ilion.
So, be their place of one estate
With ashes, echoes, and old wars,—
Or ever we be of the night,
Or we be lost among the stars.

A DESERTED VILLAGE
The wistful note this poem sounds may be autobiographical. Robinson was born in a small town in Maine that has since disappeared from most maps, and grew up in another town between Bangor and Portland. Many poor French Canadians crossed the Maine border in hard times, which may explain "strangers of another tongue" that now are found at Calverly's. It seems to be a vanished community that the poet revisits in his mind, the memory of which evokes the characters—Leffingwell, Lingard, Claverling—who once lived there.

Moon-calf = an expression sometimes used to describe a crazed or mentally retarded person.
Ilion = ancient Troy, another ruined place.

SEA-GOING

At the end of the line for the storytelling poet is the symbolic journey, where the details all have meanings on another level, where a voyage by boat becomes a metaphor for life, or death.

WALT WHITMAN, SAILOR

No, there's no mistake. This is a *short* poem by Whitman. Actually, he wrote a lot of short poems, though most of his greatest are longer. Read this as you might recite a prayer or a chant—notice how the lines get gradually longer, growing in intensity and reaching a crescendo.

ABOARD AT A SHIP'S HELM
Walt Whitman

Aboard at a ship's helm,
A young steersman steering with care.

Through fog on a sea-coast dolefully ringing,
An ocean bell—O a warning bell, rock'd by the waves.

O you give good notice indeed, you bell by the sea-reefs
    ringing,
Ringing, ringing, to warn the ship from its wreck-place.

For as on the alert O steersman, you mind the loud
    admonition,
The bows turn, the freighted ship tacking speeds away
    under her gray sails,
The beautiful and noble ship with all her precious wealth
    speeds away gayly and safe.

But O the ship, the immortal ship! O ship aboard the ship!
Ship of the body, ship of the soul, voyaging, voyaging,
    voyaging.

CROSSING THE BAR
Alfred, Lord Tennyson

Sunset and evening star,
 And one clear call for me!
And may there be no moaning of the bar,
 When I put out to sea,

But such a tide as moving seems asleep,
 Too full for sound and foam,
When that which drew from out the boundless deep
 Turns again home.

Twilight and evening bell,
 And after that the dark!
And may there be no sadness of farewell,
 When I embark;

For though from out our bourne of Time and Place
 The flood may bear me far,
I hope to see my Pilot face to face
 When I have crossed the bar.

BEYOND THE BREAKERS

Tennyson insisted that this poem, which may have been inspired by the sound of an offshore warning bell near a navigation channel, be printed last in the posthumous collections of his work. It shares with Whitman's poem a sense of the symbolic sea voyage—here the journey is outward, into eternity.

Moaning = the roar of ocean waves as they reach shallower water.
Bar = the underwater sand bar that often marks the transition from estuary to ocean, and guards safe harbors from sea waves; it's also a symbol for the line of transition from life to death.
Bourne = that which is within boundaries; in this case, life.

TRAINS AND PLANES

The storytelling poet frequently delights in conjuring far-off places. Robert Louis Stevenson's adventure stories for young readers captivated them with exotic settings and sensations, as did many of his enduringly popular poems from *A Child's Garden of Verses*. Mona Van Duyn, rather than conjuring up childlike wonder, evokes the fearful child that never quite leaves us, and shows a traveler's supposedly rational adult mind trying desperately to convince itself that nothing bad will happen.

♦ **VIEWS**
Mona Van Duyn

first poet

I fly all the time, and still I'm afraid to fly.
I need to keep both feet on the ground, the earth
within reach of my eyes. In airports I comfort myself
by assessing others—look at that handsome necktie,
the weave of that suit, the portfolio, (people of worth
are going to be on this plane) the pearls on that shelf
of expensive bosom, the hairdresser's art! All this
tells my shuddering spirit that God wouldn't tip
my seatmates, all these important people, from sight.
Once the stewardess passed the word that Liz
would be joined in Rome by Richard Burton, who was up
in First Class. I have never felt so safe on a flight.

second poet

I too fly all the time, and still I tremble.
I arrive too early and sit there sweating and cold.
I read at a book but can't make out what it means.
I look around at the others as they assemble

~60~

and make a collection of the dowdy old,
backpacking young, slouched in their dusty jeans,
men who have business suits of the wrong size on,
Frizzled Hair, Greasy Hair and Drooping Hem.
Humbly they live and humbly they will die—
this scroungiest bunch of people I've ever laid eyes on.
Surely God has no special fate in mind for them,
I tell myself, like a plane falling out of the sky.

FROM A RAILWAY CARRIAGE
Robert Louis Stevenson

Faster than fairies, faster than witches,
Bridges and houses, hedges and ditches;
And charging along like troops in a battle,
All through the meadows the horses and cattle
All of the sights of the hill and the plain
fly as thick as driving rain;
And ever again, in the wink of an eye,
Painted stations whistle by.

Here is a child who clambers and scrambles,
All by himself and gathering brambles;

ON THE CIRCUIT

This amusing poem is no joke if you fly a lot. Many contemporary poets, such as Van Duyn, earn their living flying from college campus to artist-in-residency to public reading. It's carefully and subtly rhymed, but like many modern poems it doesn't employ a strict rhythmic meter, seeking instead to reflect the sound of ordinary speech.

FASTER THAN WITCHES

Light verse and children's poems often employ bouncier rhythms inappropriate for weightier subjects. Stevenson's poem *sounds* like a railway car, and employs a meter that poets call *dactyllic*, which describes the rhythmic stress "DUM-da-da."

Here is a tramp who stands and gazes;
And there is the green for stringing the daisies!
Here is a cart run away in the road
Lumping along with man and load;
And here is a mill, and there is a river
Each a glimpse and gone for ever!

III.

POEMS OF ANIMALS AND THE NATURAL WORLD

BURDENS OF BEASTS

People will all their money to their pets, and activists are outraged more by abuses of animals than by human suffering. Apparently, we see ourselves in animals— only simpler, purer, and without all the hang-ups. Here, cats at the zoo reflect Victoria Sackville-West's sexual and artistic uncertainties. In the poem that follows, James Dickey's heaven accounts for the necessary and somehow spiritual relationship between predator and prey—in the process, perhaps, questioning our very ideas of an afterlife.

THE GREATER CATS
Victoria Sackville-West

The greater cats with golden eyes
Stare out between the bars.
Deserts are there and different skies,
And night with different stars.
They prowl the aromatic hill,
And mate as fiercely as they kill,
And hold the freedom of their will
To roam, to live, to drink their fill;
But this beyond their wit know I:
Man loves a little, and for long shall die.

Their kind across the desert range
Where tulips spring from stones,
Not knowing they will suffer change
Or vultures pick their bones.
Their strength's eternal in their sight,
They rule the terror of the night,
They overtake the deer in flight,
And in their arrogance they smite;
But I am sage, if they are strong:
Man's love is transient as his death is long.

Yet oh what powers to deceive!
My wit is turned to faith,
And at this moment I believe
In love, and scout at death.
I came from nowhere, and shall be
Strong, steadfast, swift, eternally:
I am a lion, a stone, a tree,
And as the Polar star in me
Is fixed my constant heart on thee.
Ah, may I stay forever blind
With lions, tigers, leopards, and their kind.

ALL PASSION PENT

Sackville-West, a member of the English upper class and intellectual elite who was prominent during the years between the two World Wars, was painfully aware of the straitlaced moral code expected of her. At the same time she was torn by a destructive and passionate homosexual affair. Read the poem aloud as if you were arguing with yourself: each stanza begins with images of ferocity and of the poet's passionate imagination; then—in the last two lines—it tries to moralize all that away. The repeated rhymes (such as *hill / kill / will / fill*) create a rising sense of intensity. Notice how the vivid animal images finally overwhelm the "acceptable" sentiments of the first two stanzas.

Scout = scoff.

THE HEAVEN OF ANIMALS
James Dickey

Here they are. The soft eyes open.
If they have lived in a wood
It is a wood.
If they have lived on plains
It is grass rolling
Under their feet forever.

Having no souls, they have come,
Anyway, beyond their knowing.
Their instincts wholly bloom
And they rise.
The soft eyes open.

To match them, the landscape flowers,
Outdoing, desperately
Outdoing what is required
The richest wood,
The deepest field.

For some of these,
It could not be the place
It is, without blood.

These hunt, as they have done,
But with claws and teeth grown perfect,

More deadly than they can believe.
They stalk more silently,
And crouch on the limbs of trees,
And their descent
Upon the backs of their prey

May take years
In a sovereign floating of joy.
And those that are hunted
Know this as their life,
Their reward to walk

Under such trees in full knowledge
Of what is in glory above them,
And to feel no fear,
But acceptance, compliance.
Fulfilling themselves without pain

At the cycle's center,
They tremble, they walk
Under the tree,
They fall, they are torn,
They rise, they walk again.

SOFT EYES AND CLAWS

You might call this poem "Bambi—The Dark Side." There's a tendency—particularly among those who oppose hunting—to sentimentalize and personify nature, to see the soft eyes and not the claws. Here the poet takes such sentiments to the logical extreme—a heaven of animals that would terrify "Bambi" fans. Instead of recurring rhymes and regular meter, the poem depends on recurring phrases, patterns, or thoughts for its structure. Notice how the cycles of the poem's language echo the cyclical heaven of animals.

BURDENS OF BEASTS II

Here are two famous poems in which animals take on religious significance for the poet. They're nearly polar opposites: it's the difference between a fiery evangelist preaching a hellfire sermon and a feel-good minister waxing warm and fuzzy for Jesus. Blake's poem, generally considered one of the language's greatest, lives on in literature anthologies. Alexander's lyric, meant as a children's poem, was set to music, became a favorite in the hymnal of the Anglican church, and later provided writer James Herriot with several titles for his veterinary memoirs.

THE TYGER
William Blake

Tyger! tyger! burning bright
In the forests of the night,
What immortal hand or eye
Could frame thy fearful symmetry?

In what distant deeps or skies
Burnt the fire of thine eyes?
On what wings dare he aspire?
What the hand dare seize the fire?

And what shoulder, and what art,
Could twist the sinews of thy heart?
And when thy heart began to beat,
What dread hand? and what dread feet?

What the hammer? what the chain?
In what furnace was thy brain?
What the anvil? what dread grasp
Dare it deadly terrors clasp?

When the stars threw down their spears,
And water'd heaven with their tears,
Did he smile his work to see?
Did he who made the Lamb make thee?

Tyger! Tyger! burning bright
In the forests of the night,
What immortal hand or eye
Dare frame thy fearful symmetry?

RED IN TOOTH AND CLAW
Blake's 1794 book, *Songs of Innocence and of Experience*, contrasted the innocence of youth and the experience of age. Here, instead of the innocent lamb we have the frightful tiger—the emblem of nature red in tooth and claw—that embodies experience; how can the same creator have made both? This poem is a series of questions, almost chantlike in its repetition, for which the implied answer is "God." But, for Blake, it is a frightening answer.

Aspire = rise up, soar.
What the hand (etc.) = what hand, etc., could, or would?
Twist = as fibers are twisted together to make the strands of a rope.

~69~

ALL THINGS BRIGHT AND BEAUTIFUL
Cecil Frances Alexander

All things bright and beautiful,
  All creatures great and small,
All things wise and wonderful,
  The Lord God made them all.

Each little flower that opens,
  Each little bird that sings,
He made their glowing colours,
  He made their tiny wings.

The purple-headed mountain,
  The river running by,
The sunset, and the morning,
  That brightens up the sky;

The cold wind in the winter,
    The pleasant summer sun,
The ripe fruits in the garden,
    He made them every one.

He gave us eyes to see them,
    And lips that we might tell,
How great is God Almighty,
    Who has made all things well.

HYMNS FOR LITTLE CHILDREN

Alexander's poem first appeared in her collection, *Hymns for Little Children*, written in the mid-1800s before she was married and had a family of her own. It is typical of Victorian children's poems in its determinedly upbeat and condescending tone, which is one reason why the far more playful and rascally nonsense poems of her contemporaries Edward Lear and Lewis Carroll seem more charming and less dated today. Most hymns are written in *hymnal measure* (or two variations—*short* measure and *long* measure), which alternates an unrhymed four-beat (*tetrameter*) line with a rhymed three-beat (*trimeter*) line.

WHAT SINGERS KNOW

A book of bird poetry
would include some of the
greatest poems in the
language. It's easy to see
why. There is something
ancient, something eternal
in bird songs, even though
the birds themselves live
only a few years. Poets
think of themselves
as singers too, and they
write and publish songs
that they hope will last
after the singer has gone.

Sound again = echo.
Flowers/as one to ten = there
are fewer summer flowers
than spring flowers.
Comes = soon will come.
That other fall = autumn,
the fall of leaves (instead of
the fall of flower petals).
Not to sing = the sound is a
question, not a song.

THE OVEN-BIRD
Robert Frost

There is a singer everyone has heard,
Loud, a mid-summer and a mid-wood bird,
Who makes the solid tree trunks sound again.
He says that leaves are old and that for flowers
Mid-summer is to spring as one to ten.
He says the early petal-fall is past,
When pear and cherry bloom went down in showers
On sunny days a moment overcast;
And comes that other fall we name the fall.
He says the highway dust is over all.
The bird would cease and be as other birds
But that he knows in singing not to sing.
The question that he frames in all but words
Is what to make of a diminished thing.

PROUD SONGSTERS
Thomas Hardy

The thrushes sing as the sun is going,
   And the finches whistle in ones and pairs,
And as it gets dark loud nightingales
     In bushes
Pipe, as they can when April wears,
   As if all Time were theirs.

These are brand new birds of twelve-months' growing
   Which a year ago, or less than twain
No finches were, nor nightingales,
     Nor thrushes,
But only particles of grain,
   And earth, and air, and rain.

QUESTIONS IN THE WOODS

Frost was interested in simple things that revealed complex questions; the bird's loud song in late summer sounded to him like a question. Notice how "he says" repeats, the way a bird's song does. This is a sonnet, though the interlocking rhyme pattern doesn't match the Elizabethan sonnets of Shakespeare and Spenser.

ELEMENTS OF SONG

You may have to read this several times before the structure becomes clear. Notice how *bushes*, in the first stanza, is not rhymed until *thrushes*, in the last. Read it out loud slowly, starting each stanza strongly and letting the last lines of each trail off into almost a whisper.

Twain = two.

EMBLEMATICAL CATS

Aesop knew that animal fables were a good way to make moral points. Certain animals seem to embody different parts of the human character. Cats have often been associated with femininity—in both critical and complimentary ways. Here, Thomas Gray draws an amusing, but fairly heavy-handed moral from the demise of the fair Selima. Denise Levertov, in the following poem, deliberately strips away all the emblematical baggage—fair to neither cat nor human—from the purring animal on her lap.

ODE ON THE DEATH OF A FAVORITE CAT, DROWNED IN A TUB OF GOLD FISHES
Thomas Gray

'Twas on a lofty vase's side
Where China's gayest art had dyed
    The azure flowers that blow;
Demurest of the tabby kind,
The pensive Selima reclined,
    Gazed on the lake below.

Her conscious tail her joy declared;
The fair round face, the snowy beard,
    The velvet of her paws,
Her coat, that with the tortoise vies,
Her ears of jet, and emerald eyes,
    She saw; and purred applause.

Still had she gazed; but 'midst the tide
Two angel forms were seen to glide,
    The genii of the stream:
Their scaly armour's Tyrian hue
Through richest purple to the view
    Betrayed a golden gleam.

The hapless nymph with wonder saw:
A whisker first and then a claw,
    With many an ardent wish,
She stretched in vain to reach the prize.
What female heart can gold despise?
    What cat's averse to fish?

Presumptuous maid! with looks intent
Again she stretched, again she bent,
    Nor knew the gulf between.
(Malignant Fate sat by and smiled)
The slippery verge her feet beguiled,
    She tumbled headlong in.

Eight times emerging from the flood
She mewed to every watery god,
    Some speedy aid to send.
No dolphin came, no Nereid stirred:
Nor cruel Tom nor Susan heard.
    A favourite has no friend!

ALL THAT GLISTERS

Here is another beast fable, this one with a clear—if sexually stereotyped—moral point. Selima the cat is treated as a tragic heroine, and is condescended to as a symbol of the narcissistic woman whose ambitious reach, like Eve's, leads to disaster. As with many of the poems of Gray's era, the wit and clever rhymes of the poem are much on display, and you should emphasize them when you read it out loud.

Blow = blossom.
Genii = spirits.
Tyrian hue = purple.
Nereid = sea nymph.
Glisters = glistens.

From hence, ye beauties, undeceived,
Know, one false step is ne'er retrieved.
    And be with caution bold.
Not all that tempts your wandering eyes
And heedless hearts is lawful prize.
    Nor all that glisters, gold.

THE CAT AS CAT
Denise Levertov

The cat on my bosom
sleeping and purring
—fur-petalled chrysanthemum,
squirrel-killer—

is a metaphor only if I
force him to be one,
looking too long in his pale, fond,
dilating, contracting eyes

that reject mirrors, refuse
to observe what bides
stockstill.
      Likewise

flex and reflex of claws
gently pricking through sweater to skin
gently sustains their own tune
not mine. I-Thou, cat, I-Thou.

LINES THAT PURR

Compared to Gray's cat, to which all sorts of human characteristics are attributed, Levertov's cat is a cat. Where Selima, like the mythical Narcissus, admires a reflection, the cat on Levertov's lap rejects mirrors, is interested only in motion—a much more accurate description of cat vision and psychology. It is the *poet* who sees things in the cat's eyes. This poem even *sounds* like a cat, the words chosen to reflect the rhythm of the purring, kneading animal.

Fur-petaled chrysanthemum = one possible metaphor that the poet soon rejects. *Squirrel-killer* = a description that opposes the flower image, but which is also unfair in its moral disapproval of an amoral animal.

DOGS LOVED AND LOST

Dogs are supposed to be man's best friends, and in poetry they often stand for certain male qualities—again, both the praiseworthy and the lamentable.

Prove = demonstrate, try out; She sings her lover's songs on occasion. *Clips* = clasps; she cuddles the dog. *That lap doth lap* = she lets the dog lick her. *Since wit/becomes a clog* = since his beloved seems to love witless things, he hopes love will make him lose his wits.

DEAR, WHY MAKE YOU MORE OF A DOG THAN ME?
Sir Philip Sidney

Dear, why make you more of a dog than me?

If he do love, I burn, I burn in love:

If he wait well, I never thence would move:

If he be fair, yet but a dog can be.

Little he is, so little worth is he;

He barks, my songs thine own voice oft doth prove:

Bidd'n perhaps he fetcheth thee a glove,

But I unbid, fetch even my soul to thee.

Yet while I languish, him that bosom clips,

That lap doth lap, nay lets in spite of spite,

This sour-breath'd mate taste of those sugred lips

Alas, if you grant only such delight

To witless things, then Love, I hope (since wit

Becomes a clog) will soon ease me of it.

LAMENT FOR TOBY, A FRENCH POODLE

May Sarton

The great Toby is dead,
Courteous and discreet,
He of the noble head,
Remote and tragic air,
He of the trim black feet—
He's gone. He is nowhere.

Yet famous in New Hampshire
As one who fought and killed—
Dog-bane and dog-despair—
That prey that all resign,
The terrible and quilled,
Heraldic porcupine.

He will become a legend,
Black coat and royal nature,
So wounded he was blind,
As on a painted shield
Some lost heroic creature
Who fought and would not yield.

DUMB ANIMALS

Here the ardent lover
Astrophel (the guise worn
by Sir Philip Sidney in his
sonnet sequence *Astrophel
and Stella*) sees a rival in his
beloved's lapdog. So, like
any self-respecting guy
with hair on his chest, he
must prove which is the
better man.

TILTING AT WINDMILLS

Too much macho is trouble,
apparently. Sarton's poem
is couched in the language
of heraldry—the tradition-
al elements that identify
knights, and their coats
of arms. The irony is clear.
Read it with an attitude of
fondness tempered by both
amusement and regret for
Toby, whose last battle
with a porcupine was
rather like Don Quixote's
attack upon the windmills.

If we were brave as he,
Who'd ask to be wise?
We shall remember Toby:
When human courage fails,
Be dogged in just cause
As he before the quills.

ORCHARD

H.D.

I saw the first pear
as it fell—
the honey-seeking, golden-banded,
the yellow swarm
was not more fleet than I,
(spare us from loveliness)
and I fell prostrate,
crying:
you have flayed us
with your blossoms,
spare us the beauty
of fruit-trees.

The honey-seeking
paused not,
the air thundered their song,
and I alone was prostrate.

O rough-hewn
god of the orchard,

GARDEN VARIETIES

Not only animals, but
the natural world itself be-
comes, in a poet's hands, a
symbol for human life and
society. If the Garden of
Eden was paradise, with
man and nature in harmony,
gardeners ever since have
sought to bring order to
the chaos of life. But even
in the carefully ordered
world of the garden or
orchard, the fearsome
cycle of birth and death
goes on, which perhaps
accounts for the frantic
note in the voices of the
women in these green
worlds of these poems by
H.D. and Rita Dove.

PRAYER TO PRIAPUS

H.D. (the pen name of Hilda Doolittle) helped found the school of modern poetry known as Imagism, of which this poem is a precursor. Through vivid and emotionally charged images, and verses inspired by classical models, she rejects the sentimentality and puffed-up language of Victorian poetry. This poem was originally entitled "Priapus," after the Greek god of orchards and male procreative power.

Begin as if recalling a shocking sight, then turn it into a prayer to the orchard god—a prayer mixed with despair and revulsion.

Honey-seeking = probably yellow jackets, which are drawn to rotting fruit.

I bring an offering—
do you, alone unbeautiful,
son of the god,
spare us from loveliness:

these fallen hazel-nuts,
stripped late of their green sheaths,
grapes, red-purple
their berries
dripping with wine,
pomegranates already broken,
and shrunken figs
and quinces untouched,
I bring you as offering.

CAMEOS
Rita Dove

Lucille among the flamingos
is pregnant; is pained
because she cannot stoop to pluck
the plumpest green tomato
deep on the crusted vine.

Lucille considers
the flamingos, guarding in plastic cheer
the bird bath, parched
and therefore
deserted. In her womb
a dull and husky ache.

If she picks it, Joe will come home
for breakfast tomorrow.
She will slice and dip it
in egg and cornmeal and fry
the tart and poison out.
Sobered by the aroma he'll show
for sure, and sit down

without a mumbling word.
Inconsiderate, then

the vine that languishes
so!, and the bath sighing for water
while the diffident flamingos arrange
their torchsong tutus.
She alone
is the blues. Pain drives her blank.
Lucille thinks *I can't*
even see my own feet.

Lucille lies down
between tomatoes
and the pole beans heavenly shade.
From here everything looks
reptilian. The tomato plops
in her outstretched palm. *Now*
he'll come she thinks
and it will be a son.
The birdbath hushed
behind a cloud
of canebreak and blossoming flame.

A DESCRIPTION OF A CITY SHOWER

Jonathan Swift

An Imitation of Virgil's Georgics

Careful observers may foretell the hour

(By sure prognostics) when to dread a shower:

While rain depends, the pensive cat gives o'er

Her frolics and pursues her tail no more.

Returning home at night, you'll find the sink

Strike your offended sense with double stink.

If you be wise, then go not far to dine:

You'll spend in coach-hire more than save in wine.

A coming shower your shooting corns presage,

Old aches throb, your hollow tooth will rage;

Sauntering in coffeehouse is Dulman seen;

He damns the climate, and complains of spleen.

Meanwhile the South, rising with dabbled wings,

A sable cloud athwart the welkin flings,

That swilled more liquor than it could contain,

And like a drunkard gives it up again.

Brisk Susan whips her linen from the rope,

While the first drizzling shower is borne aslope;

Such is that sprinkling which some careless quean

GREAT NATURE WRITING

As the mysteries of the world were beginning to give up some of their secrets, poets often celebrated the order and symmetry of nature with traditional poems called Georgics, that praised the natural order. Jonathan Swift, a priest in the Church of England, saw instead the ungodliness, squalor, and hypocrisy of the era. He pokes fun at such inflated poems about nature by describing the squalid urban landscape, and to give it extra bite he employs "heroic couplets," a form such poems commonly employed.

Depends = threatens.
Dulman = some unnamed "dull man."
Gives o'er = quits.

This poem describes a developing action: the first stanza describes the signs that accompany the coming of rain, the second stanza describes the first sprinkles of dirty rain, the third stanza describes the fully developed shower and the people seeking shelter from it, and the fourth stanza describes the trash that washes down the drainage ditches. The couplets force you to pay attention to the rhyme at the end of each line, and to the wit of the rhymes. Thus it's a shock when Swift concludes with the last three gory lines, which have six beats each for emphasis.

Spleen = a general term used to describe the ill spirits thought to cause sickness.
A-thwart the welkin = "across the sky," in the kind of puffed-up poetic language Swift is satirizing.
Aslope = slanting.

flirts on you from her mop, but not so clean:
You fly, invoke the gods; then, turning, stop
To rail; she singing, still whirls on her mop.
Not yet, the dust had shunned the unequal strife,
But, aided by the wind, fought still for life,
And wafted with its foe by violent gust,
'Twas doubtful which was rain and which was dust.
Ah! where must needy poet seek for aid,
When dust and rain at once his coat invade?
His only coat, where dust confused with rain,
Roughen the nap, and leave a mingled stain.

Now in contiguous drops the flood comes down,
Threatening with deluge this *devoted* town.
To shops in crowds the daggled females fly,
Pretend to cheapen goods, but nothing buy.
The Templar spruce, while every spout's abroach,
Stays till 'tis fair, yet seems to call a coach.
The tucked-up seamstress walks with hasty strides,
While streams run down her oiled umbrella's sides.
Here various kinds by various fortunes led,
Commence acquaintance underneath a shed.
Triumphant Tories, and desponding Whigs,
Forget their feuds, and join to save their wigs.

Boxed in a chair the beau impatient sits,
While spouts run clattering o'er the roof by fits;
And ever and anon with frightful din
The leather sounds; he trembles from within.
So when Troy chairmen bore the wooden steed,
Pregnant with Greeks impatient to be freed,
(Those bully Greeks, who, as the moderns do,
Instead of paying chairmen, run them through),
Laocoon struck the outside with his spear,
And each imprisoned hero quaked for fear.

   Now from all parts the swelling kennels flow,
And bear their trophies with them as they go
Filth of all hues and odours seem to tell
What street they sail'd from, by their sight and smell.
They, as each torrent drives, with rapid force
From Smithfield or St. Pulchre's shape their course,
And in huge confluent join at Snow Hill Ridge,
Fall from the conduit prone to Holborn bridge.
Sweepings from butchers' stalls, dung, guts, and blood,
Drowned puppies, stinking sprats, all drenched in mud,
Dead cats and turnip-tops come tumbling down the flood.

Quean = a disreputable
woman.
Nap = the surface of a
fabric.
Devoted = doomed.
Cheapen goods = haggle.
Templar spruce = well-
dressed Mason.
Chair = a covered and
waterproof "sedan chair"
with which two bearers
carry a wealthy passenger
(Swift here likens it to
Homer's "Trojan horse";
some unscrupulous
passengers would get out
and stab their bearers when
it came time to pay).
Laocoon = A Trojan skepti-
cal of the Greeks' "gift."
Kennels = gutters or
drainage channels.

IV.

POEMS OF CONTRADICTION AND OPPOSITION

STIRRINGS OF GREEN

Traditionally poets have sung songs to the coming of spring. The medieval French celebrated spring with a type of dance song called a *reverdie* ("greening again" after winter), that English poets from Geoffrey Chaucer onward took up with great enthusiasm. But spring is full of contradictions, and contradictions seem to attract poets even more than good weather.

Here are the opening eighteen lines of two long poems that present visions of an entire world, both of which begin with the green of spring.

For translations and notes on these poems, see page 199.

FROM THE GENERAL PROLOGUE, *THE CANTERBURY TALES*
Geoffrey Chaucer

Whan that April with his showrés soote
The droughte of March hath percéd to the roote,
And bathéd every veine in swich licour,
Of which vertu engendréd is the flowr;
Whan Zephyrus eek with his sweeté breeth
Inspiréd hath in every holt and heeth
The tendre croppés, and the yongé sonne
Hath in the Ram his halvé cours yronne,
And smalé fowlés maken melodye
That sleepen al the night with open yë—
So priketh hem Nature in her corages—
Thanne longen folk to goon on pilgrimages,
and palmeres for to seeken straungé strondes
To ferné halwés, couthe in sondry londes;
And specially from every shirés ende
Of Engélond to Canterbury they wende,
The holy blisful martyr for to seeke
That hem hath holpen whan that they were seke.

FROM THE BURIAL OF THE DEAD,
THE WASTE LAND

T. S. Eliot

April is the cruellest month, breeding

Lilacs out of the dead land, mixing

Memory and desire, stirring

Dull roots with spring rain.

Winter kept us warm, covering

Earth in forgetful snow, feeding

A little life with dried tubers.

Summer surprised us, coming over the Starnbergersee

With a shower of rain; we stopped in the colonnade,

and went on in sunlight, into the Hofgarten,

and drank coffee, and talked for an hour.

Bin gar keine Russin, stamm' aus Litauen, echt deutsch.

And when we were children, staying at the arch-duke's,

My cousin's, he took me out on a sled,

And I was frightened. He said, Marie,

Marie, hold on tight. And down we went.

In the mountains, there you feel free.

I read, much of the night, and go south in the winter.

MIDDLE ENGLISH
If you don't quite get Chaucer at first, relax. For centuries, no one else did, either. See page 199 for a translation of some of the unfamiliar Middle English words that appears in this short excerpt, and some notes on how to pronounce Middle English.

IN DIFFERENT VOICES
An early version of "The Waste Land," set in a brothel, was entitled "He Do the Police in Different Voices." Eliot cut that part out, but the poem remains a collection of voices, and even this small selection contains several. See the note on page 200 for additional background, and keys to the unfamiliar words.

The Elder Poet

Greek poets often wrote poems lamenting the death of an elder, and "better," poet. Such poems were also a way for the young poet to announce, "Watch out world, here I come."

Poets have done it ever since. For instance, early in John Milton's career he wrote "Lycidas," a tribute to the minor poet Edward King. Today, it's about the only reason anyone knows King's name. While Yeats was considered a major poet in his lifetime, this great memorial poem did nothing to diminish his stature. It didn't do the young Auden's reputation any harm, either.

In Memory of W. B. Yeats (d. Jan. 1939)
W. H. Auden

I

He disappeared in the dead of winter:
The brooks were frozen, the airports almost deserted,
And snow disfigured the public statues;
The mercury sank in the mouth of the dying day.
What instruments we have agree
The day of his death was a dark cold day.

Far from his illness
The wolves ran on through the evergreen forests,
The peasant river was untempted by the fashionable
    quays;
By mourning tongues
The death of the poet was kept from his poems.

But for him it was his last afternoon as himself,
An afternoon of nurses and rumours;
The provinces of his body revolted,
The squares of his mind were empty,
Silence invaded the suburbs,
The current of his feeling failed; he became his admirers.

Now he is scattered among a hundred cities
And wholly given over to unfamiliar affections,
To find his happiness in another kind of wood
And be punished under a foreign code of conscience.
The words of a dead man
Are modified in the guts of the living.

But in the importance and noise of to-morrow
When the brokers are roaring like beasts on the floor of
    the Bourse,
And the poor have the sufferings to which they are fairly
    accustomed,
And each in the cell of himself is almost convinced of his
    freedom,
A few thousand will think of this day
As one thinks of a day when one did something slightly
    unusual.
What instruments we have agree
The day of his death was a dark cold day.

II

You were silly like us; your gift survived it all
The parish of rich women, physical decay,
Yourself. Mad Ireland hurt you into poetry.

♦ **DEAD OF WINTER**
Actually, the weather
was pretty good in France
when Yeats died there.
The death of one old poet
on the eve of World War II
hardly seemed worth
notice, but Auden finds in
Yeats's legacy something
that endures: words that
can heal, that can change
the world in the long run.
Read the first part of the
poem as if you were telling
the story of Yeats's death
to someone who hadn't
heard the news. Address
the second part to Yeats
directly, as if you're
speaking to his departed
spirit. The last part is in
strongly rhymed, rhythmic,
memorial couplets that
you should read as if this
tribute might be carved on
his tombstone.

Provinces / squares / suburbs =
the poet is described as a
country unto himself.
Another kind of wood = this
refers to the evergreen
forests of the second stanza
—the imaginative world
created by his poems.
Bourse = French stock
market.
Rich women = Yeats's
patrons included a number
of wealthy English and
Irish women.

Now Ireland has her madness and her weather still,

For poetry makes nothing happen: it survives

In the valley of its making where executives

Would never want to tamper, flows on south

From ranches of isolation and the busy griefs,

Raw towns that we believe and die in; it survives,

A way of happening, a mouth.

III

Earth, receive an honoured guest:

William Yeats is laid to rest.

Let the Irish vessel lie

Emptied of its poetry.

In the nightmare of the dark

All the dogs of Europe bark,

And the living nations wait,

Each sequestered in its hate;

Intellectual disgrace

Stares from every human face,

And the seas of pity lie

Locked and frozen in each eye.

Follow, poet, follow right
To the bottom of the night,
With your unconstraining voice
Still persuade us to rejoice;

With the farming of a verse
Make a vineyard of the curse,
Sing of human unsuccess
In a rapture of distress;

In the deserts of the heart
Let the healing fountain start,
In the prison of his days
Teach the free man how to praise.

"Occasional poetry"—which marks an occasion or event—is full of the sort of natural contradictions that good poets depend on. Ralph Waldo Emerson's poem here seems a conventional tribute by which the poet immortalizes in verse heroes of a day gone by; but there's more to it. Nothing lasts, not even stone monuments, except the transcendant spirit. Robert Lowell, answering Emerson years later, exposes the contradictions inherent in our national myth, and the mundane reality of New England today.

The shot heard round the world = the beginning of the first great colonial revolution. *Votive* = memorial.

CONCORD HYMN

Ralph Waldo Emerson

Sung at the completion of the Battle Monument, July 4, 1837

By the rude bridge that arched the flood,
  Their flag to April's breeze unfurled,
Here once the embattled farmers stood
  And fired the shot heard round the world.

The foe long since in silence slept;
  Alike the conqueror silent sleeps;
And Time the ruined bridge has swept
  Down the dark stream which seaward creeps.

On this green bank, by this soft stream,
  We set to-day a votive stone;
That memory may their deed redeem,
  When, like our sires, our sons are gone.

Spirit, that made those heroes dare
  To die, and leave their children free,
Bid Time and Nature gently spare
  The shaft we raise to them and thee.

CONCORD
Robert Lowell

Ten thousand Fords are idle here in search
Of a tradition. Over these dry sticks—
The Minute Man, the Irish Catholics,
The ruined bridge and Walden's fished-out perch—
The belfry of the Unitarian Church
Rings out the hanging Jesus. Crucifix,
How can your whited spindling arms transfix
Mammon's unbridled industry, the lurch
For forms to harness Heraclitus' stream!
This Church is Concord—Concord where Thoreau
Named all the birds without a gun to probe
Through darkness to the painted man and bow:
The death-dance of King Philip and his scream
Whose echo girdled this imperfect globe.

THE RIVALS

Politicians get elected by "defining the opponent." Poets sometimes use the same strategy, defining themselves by other poets or writers they oppose. It can get brutal: poets have many enemies, real and imagined. What greater measure of fame exists, after all, than making a hated rival look foolish for all of time? In these two poems, Alexander Pope and Howard Nemerov let fly at rivals. (One final point: the editor of this book would like to take this occasion to apologize to every poet, living and dead, whose work is not included here —as well as to those whose work *is*.)

ATTICUS

Alexander Pope

If meagre Gildon draws his venal quill,
I wish the man a dinner, and sit still;
If Dennis rhymes, and raves in furious fret,
I'll answer Dennis, when I am in debt:
Hunger, not malice, makes such authors print,
And who'll wage war with Bedlam or the mint?
But were there one whom better stars conspire
To bless, whom Titan touch'd with purer fire,
Was form'd to write, converse, and live, with ease:
Should such a man, too fond of rule alone,
Bear, like the Turk, no brother near the throne;
View him with scornful, yet with jealous eyes,
And hate, for arts that caus'd himself to rise;
Damn with faint praise, assent with civil leer,
And without sneering, teach the rest to sneer;
Or pleas'd to wound, and yet afraid to strike,
Just hint a fault, and hesitate dislike;
Alike reserv'd to blame or to commend,
A tim'rous foe and a suspitious friend:

Fearing ev'n fools, by flatterers besieg'd;

And so obliging, that he ne'er oblig'd:

Who when two wits on rival themes contest,

Approves them both, but likes the worst the best:

Like Cato, gives his little senate laws,

And sits attentive to his own applause;

While fops and templars ev'ry sentence raise,

And wonder with a foolish face of praise:

What pity, heav'n! if such a man there be?

Who would not weep, if Addison were he?

FAINT PRAISE

Pope grew to hate Joseph Addison, whom he called "the English Atticus," after a classical Roman bookseller and writer. Like a nightclub comedian, ready to ridicule anyone who heckles him, Pope was feared in his day as a master of the put-down.

Gildon / Dennis = Charles Gildon and John Dennis, two contemporaries frequently strapped for money.
Bedlam = Bethlehem asylum.
The mint = a debtor's sanctuary in London; not a currency mint.
Titan = the sun.
The Turk = the Ottoman kings were said to kill all rivals to the throne, including their brothers.
Cato = Addison had written a play about the Roman senator Cato, which Pope had praised before the feud began.

NOVELISTS
Howard Nemerov

Theirs is a trade for egomaniacs,
People whose parents did not love them well.
It's done by wasps and women, Jews and Blacks,
In every isolation ward in Hell.

They spend their workadays imagining
What never happened and what never will
To people who are not and whose non-being
Always depends on the next syllable.

It's strange, and little wonder it makes them so
Whose lives are spun out talking to themselves
In allegories of themselves that go
Down on the paper like dividing cells

That form in communes and make colonies
And do each other in by love and hate
And generally enact the ceremonies
Intended to harmonize freedom and fate

Among the creatures and in the writer's soul.
The writer's soul? It's as if one abyss
Primps at the other's mirror and the whole
Shebang hangs fire while the lovers kiss.

HACKS

Before you take the invective here too seriously, you should know that Nemerov, himself Jewish, was also the author of three novels. However, his irritation at the commercial success of novelists, in recent years, when the commercial market for original poetry was drying up, is likely genuine. As in Pope's poem, the wit and barbed language here make a very effective insult when read aloud. This was probably intended to be read to (or by) novelists, or audiences with novelists in them, in an attempt to rile them.

Cells/Colonies = the implication is that novelists are like amoebas and insects, but these are also puns on revolutionary "cells" and writers' "colonies," where artists feed off of one another's creativity.

BOYS AND MEN

It's said that men *will* be boys. Not only has this truth helped sell red sports cars, it has produced some wonderful poetry. Here, William Wordsworth boils down to its essence an idea that underlies some of his greatest poems, including *The Prelude*, and "Ode: Intimations of Immortality."

C. K. Williams, on the other hand, finds the idea of the child within the man to be a rather unsettling opposition—one that seems likely to give him no peace in years to come.

MY HEART LEAPS UP
William Wordsworth

My heart leaps up when I behold

A Rainbow in the sky

So was it when my life began;

So is it now I am a Man;

So be it when I shall grow old,

    Or let me die!

The Child is Father of the Man;

And I could wish my days to be

Bound each to each by natural piety.

THE WORLD'S GREATEST TRICYCLE-RIDER

C. K. Williams

The world's greatest tricycle-rider
is in my heart, riding like a wildman,
no hands, almost upside down along
the walls and over the high curbs
and stoops, his bell rapid firing,
the sun spinning in his spokes like a flame.

But he is growing older. His feet,
overshoot the pedals. His teeth set
too hard against the jolts, and I am afraid
that what I've kept from him is what
tightens his fingers on the rubber grips
and drives him again and again on the same block.

NATURAL PIETY

Wordsworth said poets should write "in the language really used by men" (and sometimes even practiced what he preached). Though a complex idea underlies this simple poem, note the absence here of elevated or archaic "poetic" language.

Natural piety = loyalty to the child that is his "father."

LIKE A WILDMAN

Modern *accentual verse* counts stresses, but not syllables. Reading Williams's poem aloud, emphasize the important words, as you would in everyday speech: "The WORLD's GREATest TRIcycle RIder/is IN my HEART, RIding like a WILDman." Though there's no regular meter, there is a pattern—four stresses per line, with an extra stress in the final line.

GIRLS AND WOMEN

An American proverb tells us that "a woman is as old as she looks, but a man is never old till he quits looking." The basic injustice of this—of the premium that society places on a woman's physical beauty and vigor—makes it a particularly powerful subject for poetry by women. Here, Alice Meynell, writing early in her career, imagines what lies ahead in a world that does not suffer its women to grow old. In the following poem, Julia Randall, looking back on a long career and at poets eternally young in their verse, finds herself somehow renewed as she follows in their footsteps.

A LETTER FROM A GIRL TO HER OWN OLD AGE
Alice Meynell

Listen, and when thy hand this paper presses,
O time-worn woman, think of her who blesses
What thy thin fingers touch, with her caresses.

O mother, for the weight of years that break thee!
O daughter, for slow time must yet awake thee,
And from the changes of my heart must make thee!

O fainting traveler, morn is gray in heaven.
Dost thou remember how the clouds were driven?
And are they calm about the fall of even?

Pause near the ending of thy long migration;
For this one sudden hour of desolation
Appeals to one hour of thy meditation.

Suffer, O silent one, that I remind thee
Of the great hills that stormed the sky behind thee,
Of the wild winds of power that have resigned thee.

Know that the mournful plain where thou must wander
Is but a gray and silent world; but ponder
The misty mountains of the morning yonder.

Listen:—the mountain winds with rain were fretting,
And sudden gleams the mountain-tops besetting.
I cannot let thee fade to death, forgetting.

What part of this wild heart of mine I know not
Will follow with thee where the great winds blow not,
And where the young flowers of the mountain grow not.

Yet let my letter with thy lost thoughts in it
Tell what the way was when thou didst begin it,
And win with thee the goal when thou shalt win it.

I have not writ this letter of divining
To make a glory of thy silent pining,
A triumph of thy mute and strange declining.

Only one youth, and the bright life was shrouded;
Only one morning, and the day was clouded;
And one old age with all regrets is crowded.

POETRY OF SENTIMENT

Despite Wordsworth's call for "language really used by men," poets in the nineteenth century usually felt they had to treat serious subjects with elaborate, poetic language. Alice Meynell, mostly forgotten today, here both celebrates youth and quarrels with the unfairness of its loss through aging. Meynell employs conventionally elevated poetic diction—*thy*, *thee*, *O*, and so forth—designed to help give her poem a serious, almost prayerlike quality. Despite some weeping and hyperbole, Meynell was better than most at avoiding the excesses of sentiment. Notice the unusual triple rhyme, which has a repetitive, driving quality.

Even = evening.

O hush, O hush! Thy tears my words are steeping.
O hush, hush, hush! So full, the fount of weeping?
Poor eyes, so quickly moved, so near to sleeping?

Pardon the girl; such strange desires beset her.
Poor woman, lay aside the mournful letter
That breaks thy heart; the one who wrote, forget her:

The one who now thy faded features guesses,
With filial fingers thy gray hair caresses,
With morning tears thy mournful twilight blesses.

To W.B.Y.
Julia Randall

I laughed, old Yeats, at your old-age desire
to bring back all your vigor. We all wish
that we could keep the savor with the dish.
I've given away bed-roll and boot.
Not Camelback, Katahdin, or Pine Butte
will I climb again. I think of those Victorian gentlemen
at 80 ready to attack
any odd Swiss or Scottish peak, even Nepal. Ah well,

they kept in good condition,

as you kept poetry, despite some crazy

notion to have it both ways,

the Celtic legend and the London news.

So I've given up

hiking, and the rare companion

even of dog-walks, much less bed and board.

I should be blessed if I could keep the word,

though it make nothing happen—but it made us

happen, and by passionate conception. I could name a few

that I've been daughter to, though they were dead

before I stirred—those toga'd, those be-wigged,

or dog-collared, or blind,

those hymn-singers, those lovers I call friend.

In the public way,

I talk and jostle; in the common plot

take this one's hand, and that one's coat,

but my halt foot

is up Helvellyn, following the great

hill-walkers. Mile by mile

I wilt, I falter. But they never fail.

HILL-WALKERS

Here one older poet is
speaking to another.
The aging Yeats went to
extremes—even undergo-
ing quackish surgery that
promised to rejuvenate
him sexually. Despite it
all, he wrote much of his
best poetry after age fifty.
Here, near seventy herself,
Julia Randall tries to put
her own long career
in perspective and take
comfort from Yeats and
other poets whose words
have lasted. Randall's
poem rhymes irregularly
and subtly. Some, such as
wish / dish, boot / Butte, are
obvious. But, in general,
the rhymes here serve
mainly to lend additional
resonance to certain lines.

Camelback, Katahdin,
Pine Butte = American
mountains.
Helvellyn = a famous moun-
tain in northern England
near Grasmere;
Wordsworth, Keats, and
other writers of their era
were passionate hikers and
hill-walkers.

POST-MORTEMS

Though we often define
ourselves by what we're
not, the difficult question
of what we *are* remains.
Here, two disquieting
poems seek in death the
essence of life. For Emily
Dickinson, the sight of
bodies arrayed at a funeral
brings to mind the living
poet's own sense of a
terrible timelessness, of
distance and separation
from the world. Sharon
Olds, watching her father
die, turns to exact—
even clinical—description
at a terribly emotional
moment, trying somehow
to capture the mystery of
what gave him identity.

IT WAS NOT DEATH, FOR I STOOD UP
Emily Dickinson

It was not Death, for I stood up,
And all the Dead, lie down—
It was not Night, for all the Bells
Put out their Tongues, for Noon.

It was not Frost, for on my flesh
I felt Siroccos—crawl—
Nor fire—for just my Marble feet
Could keep a Chancel, cool—

And yet, it tasted, like them all,
The figures I have seen
Set orderly, for Burial,
Reminded me, of mine—

As if my life were shaven,
And fitted to a frame,
And could not breathe without a key,
And 'twas like Midnight, some—

When everything that ticked—has stopped—
And Space stares all around—
Or Grisly frosts—first Autumn morns,
Repeal the Beating Ground—

But, most, like Chaos—Stopless—cool—
Without a Chance, or Spar—
Or even a Report of Land—
To justify—Despair.

THE YELLOW ROSE OF AMHERST

By turns morbid, frenzied, bitter, philosophical, grieving, ecstatic: the enigmatic Emily may ultimately be the most notable of all American poets, in part because so much of her reclusive life is lived out in poems so unmistakable that any imitation becomes parody. It's said that you can sing any Dickinson poem to the tune of "The Yellow Rose of Texas." Now, put that completely out of your mind.

Tongues = clappers.
Siroccos = hot African winds.
Chancel = the space near the altar of a church, often made of stone.
Shaven = a carpenter's term, referring here to coffin wood.
Grisly = gray.
Repeal = the frost here takes away the life that springs from the earth.
Spar = floating remnant of a shipwreck.

THE MOMENT OF MY FATHER'S DEATH
Sharon Olds

When he breathed his last breath it was he,
my father, although he was so transformed
no one who had not been with him
for the last hours would know him, the gold
skin luminous as cold animal fat,
the eyes cast all the way back into his head,
the whites gleaming like a white iris, the
nose that grew thinner and thinner every minute, the
open mouth racked open with that
tongue in it like all the heartbreak of the mortal,
a tongue so dried, scalloped, darkened and
material. You could see the mucus
risen like gorge into the back of his mouth
but it was he, the huge slack yellow arms,
the spots of blood under the skin
black and precise, we had come this far with him
step by step, it was he, his last
breath was his, not taken with desire but
his, light as the sphere of a dandelion seed
coming out of his mouth and floating across the room.

Then the nurse pulled up his gown and
listened for his heart, I saw his stomach
silvery and hairy, it was his stomach, she
moved to the foot of the bed and stood there, she
did not shake her head she stood and
nodded at me. And for a minute it was fully
he, my father, dead but completely
himself, a man with an open mouth and
no breath, gold skin and
black spots on his arms, I kissed him and
spoke to him. He looked like someone
killed in a violent bloodless struggle, all that
strain in his neck, that look of pulling back, that
stillness he seemed to be holding at first and
then it was holding him, the skin
tightened slightly around his whole body
as if the purely physical were claiming him,
and then it was not my father,
it was not a man, it was not an animal, I
stood and ran my hand through the silver hair,
plunged my fingers into it gently and
lifted them up slowly through the grey
waves of it, the unliving glistening
matter of this world.

EXACT DESCRIPTION
Compare Olds's poem to
Auden's "In Memory of
W. B. Yeats," where the
body dies but the poems
have a life of their own.
Not here. What makes
this poem so shocking is
the contrast between the
horrifically exact descrip-
tion of a dying body and
the repeated moments, the
phrase "it was he," when
the poet breaks in and
monitors his vital signs,
almost like an electronic
device beeping at his bed-
side. Then the line goes
flat, and you realize what
she's *not* saying.

LIGHT AND DARKNESS

Summer and winter, youth and age—opposites often define each other. Usually this means that one (rather arbitrarily) gets valued over the other: right is adroit, left is gauche. Ever since day was separated from night, darkness has gotten bad press. In the following two poems, John Milton, going blind as he prepares to write *Paradise Lost*, finds himself forced to see something else in the darkness, while Dylan Thomas can see nothing at all.

Talent = a measure of gold; subject of a famous Bible parable. Milton plays on the modern meaning too, wondering if he's up to writing a great poem. *Thousands* = angels. *Post* = hurry.

WHEN I CONSIDER HOW MY LIGHT IS SPENT
John Milton

When I consider how my light is spent,
Ere half my days, in this dark world and wide,
And that one talent which is death to hide
Lodged with me useless, though my soul more bent
To serve therewith my maker, and present
My true account, lest he, returning, chide.
"Doth God exact day-labour, light denied?"
I fondly ask; but Patience, to prevent
That murmur, soon replies "God doth not need
Either man's work or his own gifts; who best
Bear his mild yoke, they serve him best; his state
Is kingly—thousands at his bidding speed
And post o'er land and ocean without rest
They also serve who only stand and wait."

Do Not Go Gentle into that Good Night

Dylan Thomas

Do not go gentle into that good night,
Old age should burn and rave at close of day;
Rage, rage against the dying of the light.

Though wise men at their end know dark is right,
Because their words had forked no lightning they
Do not go gentle into that good night.

Good men, the last wave by, crying how bright
Their frail deeds might have danced in a green bay,
Rage, rage against the dying of the light.

Wild men who caught and sang the sun in flight,
And learn, too late, they grieved it on its way,
Do not go gentle into that good night.

Grave men, near death, who see with blinding sight
Blind eyes could blaze like meteors and be gay,
Rage, rage against the dying of the light.

FIGHT TO THE DEATH

Thomas here urges his dying father to fight to the last. It's probably the finest example in English of the *villanelle*, a nineteen-line poem with only two rhymes that repeats certain lines in a tightly structured sequence. This repetition creates remarkable emotional intensity, as each new stanza repeats and builds on the one before it.

Forked no lightning = not accomplished what they wished.
Blind eyes = perhaps a reference to Milton's poem.

And you, my father, there on the sad height,

Curse, bless, me now with your fierce tears, I pray.

Do not go gentle into that good night.

Rage, rage against the dying of the light.

V.

POEMS OF VISION

DESERT VISIONS

Among most primitive cultures, including tribes that were ancestors of most modern European cultures, the idea of the poet as one who sees hidden things has remained a powerful one. Even in modern times poets have often put on the guise of seer and interpreter. Here, in poems by Shelley and Yeats, are two examples in which the poets experience a startling moment of vision, where hidden worlds are suddenly revealed.

Mockt = imitated (but also ridiculed); the sculptor sought to deride the emotions of lesser humans in his eternal tribute, but it appears as if Time gets the last laugh.

OZYMANDIAS
Percy Bysshe Shelley

I met a traveler from an antique land
Who said: "Two vast and trunkless legs of stone
Stand in the desert. Near them, on the sand,
Half sunk, a shattered visage lies, whose frown,
And wrinkled lip, and sneer of cold command,
Tell that its sculptor well those passions read
Which yet survive, stamped on these lifeless things,
The hand that mockt them and the heart that fed;
And on the pedestal these words appear
'My name is Ozymandias, king of kings.
Look on my works, ye Mighty, and despair!'
Nothing beside remains. Round the decay
Of that colossal wreck, boundless and bare
The lone and level sands stretch far away."

THE SECOND COMING
W. B. Yeats

Turning and turning in the widening gyre

The falcon cannot hear the falconer;

Things fall apart; the centre cannot hold;

Mere anarchy is loosed upon the world,

The blood-dimmed tide is loosed, and everywhere

The ceremony of innocence is drowned;

The best lack all conviction, while the worst

Are full of passionate intensity.

Surely some revelation is at hand;

Surely the Second Coming is at hand.

The Second Coming! Hardly are those words out

When a vast image out of Spiritus Mundi

Troubles my sight: somewhere in sands of the desert

A shape with lion body and the head of a man

A gaze blank and pitiless as the sun,

Is moving its slow thighs, while all about it

Reel shadows of the indignant desert birds.

The darkness drops again; but now I know

That twenty centuries of stony sleep

TRAFFIC IN ANTIQUITIES
Classical sources actually record a statue of an Egyptian king, possibly Ramses II, with a similar inscription on it. Shelley wrote the poem not long after the discovery of the Rosetta Stone, at a time when traffic in Egyptian antiquities was brisk, and provided a sudden vision of human insignificance.

THINGS FALL APART
Watch out. Here's one of the most famous short poems of the twentieth century—W. B. Yeats's cry of alarm at the dawning of the modern era. It's a wild ride. The note on page 202 may help put it in context. A good way to read this poem would be the same way you might try to describe a nightmare to someone.

Widening gyre = an open-ended spiral upwards and outwards.

Mere = sheer.

Blood-dimmed tide = the image is that of a wave of blood.

Ceremony of innocence = organized religion, for example.

Spiritus Mundi = the soul of the universe, similar to what psychologist C. G. Jung called "the collective unconscious"; images from it are sometimes visible to the poet or seer.

Lion body = Sphinx.

Twenty centuries = Yeats believed that a new age dawned every 2,000 years.

Rocking cradle = the beginning of the Christian era.

Were vexed to nightmare by a rocking cradle,

And what rough beast, its hour come round at last,

Slouches towards Bethlehem to be born?

DOVER BEACH
Matthew Arnold

The sea is calm to-night.
The tide is full, the moon lies fair
Upon the Straits;—on the French coast, the light
Gleams and is gone; the cliffs of England stand,
Glimmering and vast, out in the tranquil bay.
Come to the window, sweet is the night air!
Only, from the long line of spray
Where the ebb meets the moon-blanch'd land,
Listen! you hear the grating roar
Of pebbles which the waves suck back, and fling,
At their return, up the high strand,
Begin, and cease, and then again begin,
With tremulous cadence slow, and bring
The eternal note of sadness in.

Sophocles long ago
Heard it on the Aegean, and it brought
Into his mind the turbid ebb and flow
Of human misery; we
find also in the sound a thought,
Hearing it by this distant northern sea.

DOUBT AND FAITH

Is the visionary poet a true seer, or just suffering from delusions? Publication of Charles Darwin's works on evolution and natural selection caused poets, like nearly everyone else, to reexamine their beliefs at a time when the "facts" of organized religion were constantly being contradicted. In the following two poems, Matthew Arnold realizes his loss of faith, and the lack of anything substantial to replace it, while an ecstatic Gerard Manley Hopkins's discovers God in the tiny details of everyday life and the daily marvels of sunset and sunrise.

Arnold wrote at a time when intellectuals were choosing up sides in the great debate, and it is a cry of doubt. Read "Dover Beach" slowly. A line such as "tremulous cadence slow" should echo the sound of waves on a rocky shore. The rhymes here are complicated and sub- tle, with as many as three or four lines between rhyming words, so don't over-emphasize them—let the connections sneak up on your listeners.

Shingle = the rocky beaches that line the English Channel. *Sophocles* = Arnold refers to Sophocles' *Antigone* and *Oedipus at Colonnus*, poems about the doomed king Oedipus. *Darkling* = dwindling light.

The Sea of Faith
Was once, too, at the full, and round earth's shore
Lay like the folds of a bright girdle furl'd.
But now I only hear
Its melancholy, long, withdrawing roar,
Retreating, to the breath
Of the night-wind, down the vast edges drear
And naked shingles of the world.

Ah, love, let us be true
To one another! for the world, which seems
To lie before us like a land of dreams,
So various, so beautiful, so new,
Hath really neither joy, nor love, nor light,
Nor certitude, nor peace, nor help for pain;
And we are here as on a darkling plain
Swept with confused alarms of struggle and flight,
Where ignorant armies clash by night.

GOD'S GRANDEUR
Gerard Manley Hopkins

The world is charged with the grandeur of God.
It will flame out, like shining from shook foil;
It gathers to a greatness, like the ooze of oil
Crushed. Why do men then now not reck his rod?
Generations have trod, have trod, have trod;
And all is seared with trade; bleared, smeared with toil;
And wears man's smudge and shares man's smell: the
soil
Is bare now, nor can foot feel, being shod.

And for all this, nature is never spent;
There lives the dearest freshness deep down things;
And though the last lights off the black West went
Oh, morning, at the brown brink eastward, springs—
Because the Holy Ghost over the bent
World broods with warm breast and with ah! bright
wings.

BRIGHT WINGS
Modern poets find Hopkins important for precisely the same reason that some readers find his poems "hard"—he sometimes breaks lines in the middle of sentences or words, or chops out words, so that a phrase like "deep down inside of things" becomes *deep down things*. A Hopkins poem often rhymes *inside* the line as well as at the end—and employs complex forms of *alliteration*: rhyming sounds at the beginnings of words (*world broods/warm breath*). Read it slowly, and notice how often sounds echo each other.

Charged = suffused, as water fills a sponge.
Flame out = flash.
Crushed = as olive oil is made.
Reck = "reckon," or "pay attention to."

EPIPHANIES

Epiphany is a religious term describing the showing forth of a divine being. The novelist James Joyce first gave the word a literary use, describing moments of intuition or perception of the physical world. It remains a useful word for conveying a certain moment of poetic vision.

Leafy-with-love = possibly the English plant called Love—*Clematis vitalba*, also known as Love-bind, Traveler's Joy, or Virgin's Bower.
Ad lib = Kavanagh uses this familiar verb as a noun here, suggesting "spontaneous ability."

CANAL BANK WALK
Patrick Kavanagh

Leafy-with-love banks and the green waters of the
    canal
Pouring redemption for me, that I do
The will of God, allow in the habitual, the banal,
Grow with nature again as before I grew.
The bright stick trapped, the breeze adding a third
Party to the couple kissing on an old seat,
And a bird gathering materials for the nest for the Word
Eloquently new and abandoned to its delirious beat.
O unworn world enrapture me, enrapture me in a web
Of fabulous grass and eternal voices by a beech,
Feed the gaping need of my senses, give me ad lib
To pray unselfconsciously with overflowing speech
For this soul needs to be honoured with a new dress
    woven
From green and blue things and arguments that cannot be
    proven.

AS ON A DARKLING PLAIN
Henry Taylor

The years pile up, but there rides with you still,
across old fields to which you have come back
to invent your home and cultivate the knack
of dying slowly, to contest your will
toward getting death behind you, to find a hill
where you can stop and let the reins go slack
and parse the dark swerve of the zodiac,
a face whose eyes find ways to hold you still.

They hold you now. You turn the chestnut mare
toward the next hill darkening to the west
and stop again. The eyes will sometimes change,
but they ride with you, glimmering and vast
as the sweet country you lost once, somewhere
between the Blue Ridge and the Wasatch Range.

♦ AD LIB
Kavanagh rejected religion in his youth. Following a serious illness in 1955, he underwent a profound religious experience while walking along a canal.

MAN ON HORSEBACK
The title of Taylor's sonnet echoes "Dover Beach"; here the poet has a vision of something precious irretrievably lost, but which he cannot forget. Notice how the two lines that end with "still" form a frame for his recollections.

Parse = the process of figuring out the grammar of a sentence.
Blue Ridge . . . Wasatch Range = the heartland of the United States, between the Appalachians and the western Rockies.

TREASURE HUNTING

We live by myths, whether we're aware of them or not—stories that our culture tells to help us explain who we are and where we come from. They extend into the lives of our families, and into our private selves. Sometimes they can be hard stories to live by. And then, suddenly, some unexpected thing—like an old shipwreck encountered on a diving expedition—embodies what we feel. Here, the poet has a vision that reveals the mythology of her own life and the culture in which she lives, and begins the slow process of exploring the powerful hold that these things have on her.

DIVING INTO THE WRECK
Adrienne Rich

First having read the book of myths,
and loaded the camera,
and checked the edge of the knife-blade,
I put on
the body-armor of black rubber
the absurd flippers
the grave and awkward mask.
I am having to do this
not like Cousteau with his
assiduous team
aboard the sun-flooded schooner
but here alone.

There is a ladder.
The ladder is always there
hanging innocently
close to the side of the schooner.
We know what it is for,
we who have used it.
Otherwise

it's a piece of maritime floss
some sundry equipment.

I go down.
Rung after rung and still
the oxygen immerses me
the blue light
the clear atoms
of our human air.
I go down.
My flippers cripple me,
I crawl like an insect down the ladder
and there is no one
to tell me when the ocean
will begin.

first the air is blue and then
it is bluer and then green and then
black I am blacking out and yet
my mask is powerful
it pumps my blood with power
the sea is another story
the sea is not a question of power
I have to learn alone

♦ SOLO DESCENT

The subject of many of
Rich's best poems is self-
exploration. Solo diving is
quite risky, particularly
into a wreck, where all
sorts of snags and traps
await. So this dive is one
into both physical and
spiritual danger, to a place
where a moment of vision
is possible. It begins by
describing how one enters
the sea; then, once the
poet leaves the safety of
the ladder, she becomes
disoriented—and the
language becomes urgent,
confused; finally, remind-
ing herself why she came,
she reorients herself and
descends to the wreck
itself.

to turn my body without force
in the deep element.

And now: it is easy to forget
what I came for
among so many who have always
lived here
swaying their crenellated fans
between the reefs
and besides
you breathe differently down here.

I came to explore the wreck.
The words are purposes.
The words are maps.
I came to see the damage that was done
and the treasures that prevail.
I stroke the beam of my lamp
slowly along the flank
of something more permanent
than fish or weed

the thing I came for:
the wreck and not the story of the wreck

the thing itself and not the myth
the drowned face always staring
toward the sun
the evidence of damage
worn by salt and sway into this threadbare beauty
the ribs of the disaster
curving their assertion
among the tentative haunters.

This is the place.
And I am here, the mermaid whose dark hair
streams black, the merman in his armored body
We circle silently
about the wreck
we dive into the hold.
I am she I am he

whose drowned face sleeps with open eyes
whose breasts still bear the stress
whose silver, copper, vermeil cargo lies
obscurely inside barrels
half-wedged and left to rot
we are the half-destroyed instruments
that once held to a course

Drowned face = the wreck itself, symmetrical like a face, and perhaps evocative of a famous song from Shakespeare's *The Tempest*: "Full fathom five thy father lies/Of his bones are coral made/Those are pearls that were his eyes/Nothing of him that doth fade.

the water-eaten log
the fouled compass

We are, I am, you are
by cowardice or courage
the one who find our way
back to this scene
carrying a knife, a camera
a book of myths
in which
our names do not appear.

THE GOOD MAN IN HELL
Edwin Muir

I f a good man were ever housed in Hell
   By needful error of the qualities,
Perhaps to prove the rule or shame the devil,
   Or speak the truth only a stranger sees,

Would he, surrendering quick to obvious hate,
   fill half eternity with cries and tears,
Or watch beside Hell's little wicket gate
   In patience for the first ten thousand years,

Feeling the curse climb slowly to his throat
   That, uttered, dooms him to rescindless ill,
Forcing his praying tongue to run by rote,
   Eternity entire before him still?

Would he at last, grown faithful in his station,
   Kindle a little hope in hopeless Hell,
And sow among the damned doubts of damnation,
   Since here someone could live and could live well?

NIGHTMARES AND DREAMS

The following poems are
two visions of pent-up rage.
Langston Hughes manages
to crystallize in a few vivid
images the pent-up feelings
of racial injustice and bit-
terness that would ignite
like bombs in the 1960s
and the 1990s. Edwin
Muir, who grew up in the
working-class slums of
Glasgow, Scotland, could
perhaps afford to be more
philosophical, but his vision
of hope in the face of hope-
lessness is nevertheless
enchanting.

ITS OWN PLACE

Several of Muir's poems deal with the classical myths of heroes descending to the underworld. In Milton's *Paradise Lost*, one of the fallen Satan's famous lines is "The mind is its own place, and in itself/Can make a heaven of hell, a hell of heaven." Muir's good man seems to answer him.

A HEAVY LOAD

Compare this poem to Nikki Giovanni's "Master Charge Blues," and you'll notice that it resembles a blues lyric, though not as directly as Giovanni's. Hughes often sought to capture the spirit of blues lyrics in his poems. The last question should be almost a hiss.

One doubt of evil would bring down such a grace,

Open such a gate, all Eden could enter in,

Hell be a place like any other place,

And love and hate and life and death begin.

DREAM DEFERRED
Langston Hughes

What happens to a dream deferred?

Does it dry up

like a raisin in the sun?

Or fester like a sore—

And then run?

Does it stink like rotten meat?

Or crust and sugar over—

like a syrupy sweet?

maybe it just sags

like a heavy load.

Or does it explode?

ODE ON MELANCHOLY
John Keats

I

N o, no! go not to Lethe, neither twist
    Wolf's Bane, tight-rooted, for its poisonous wine;
Nor suffer thy pale forehead to be kiss'd
    By nightshade, ruby grape of Proserpine;
Make not your rosary of yew-berries,
    Nor let the beetle, or the death-moth be
        Your mournful Psyche, nor the downy owl
A partner in your sorrow's mysteries;
    For shade to shade will come too drowsily
        And drown the wakeful anguish of the soul.

II

But when the melancholy fit shall fall
    Sudden from heaven like a weeping cloud,
That fosters the droop-headed flowers all,
    And hides the green hill in an April shroud;
Then glut thy sorrow on a morning rose,
    Or on the rainbow of the salt-sand wave,
        Or on the wealth of globed peonies;

MELANCHOLISM

A recent popular song suggests that to get to heaven you have to "go through hell." The idea that you can't appreciate the good without the bad is an idea that's been around awhile. For some poets, though, it was fashionable to affect a pose of constant sorrow and melancholy—a pretense that John Keats scoffs at here. It is in *sudden* sadness that one appreciates joy, in death that one sees beauty. And, in the following poem, that's just the sort of vision that comes to John Crowe Ransom watching the dark comedy of little Janet and her pet chicken.

This poem may have been aimed at some of Keats's contemporaries and predecessors who acted the part of the Melancholy Poet as a way of seeming "deep." Read it aloud as if you were giving someone friendly advice—advice that leads to a wrenching realization.

Lethe = the river of forgetfulness in Hades.
Wolfs-Bane / Nightshade = poisonous plants.
Proserpine = queen of the underworld.
Yew = berries traditionally symbolic of death.
Psyche = the goddess' name also means breath, or life itself; another meaning is "butterfly," or "moth," both of which were images of the soul.
Mysteries = secrets; secret rites.
She = the goddess of Melancholy.
Fine = discerning.

Or if thy mistress some rich anger shows,

   Emprison her soft hand, and let her rave,

     And feed deep, deep upon her peerless eyes.

III

She dwells with Beauty—Beauty that must die;

   And Joy, whose hand is ever at his lips

Bidding adieu; and aching Pleasure nigh,

   Turning to poison while the bee-mouth sips

Ay, in the very temple of Delight

   Veil'd Melancholy has her sovran shrine,

     Though seen of none save him whose strenuous tongue

   Can burst Joy's grape against his palate fine;

His soul shall taste the sadness of her might,

   And be among her cloudy trophies hung.

JANET WAKING
John Crowe Ransom

Beautifully Janet slept
Till it was deeply morning. She woke then
And thought about her dainty-feathered hen,
To see how it had kept.

One kiss she gave her mother.
Only a small one gave she to her daddy
Who would have kissed each curl of his shining baby;
No kiss at all for her brother.

"Old Chucky, old Chucky!" she cried,
Running across the world upon the grass
To Chucky's house, and listening. But alas,
Her Chucky had died.

It was a transmogrifying bee
Came droning down on Chucky's old bald head
And sat and put the poison. It scarcely bled,
But how exceedingly

TRANSMOGRIFICATION
Ransom takes what could be a maudlin and sentimental subject and makes it both funny and touching. His rhymed verse adds formality to a sentiment that could overwhelm such a subject—after you read the first line of each stanza, the couplet of the second and third lines rhymes strongly, allowing the final line of each stanza to sneak back up on you, echoing the rhyme of the first. In all but the last stanza the rhyme has the effect of an afterthought. By the poem's close we're focusing not on Janet, but on the poet, and like him we can only watch Janet helplessly.

Transmogrifying = having the power to suddenly change things, often grotesquely.

And purply did the knot
Swell with the venom and communicate
Its rigor! Now the poor comb stood up straight
But Chucky did not.

So there was Janet
Kneeling on the wet grass, crying her brown hen
(Translated far beyond the daughters of men)
To rise and walk upon it.

And weeping fast as she had breath
Janet implored us, "Wake her from her sleep!"
And would not be instructed in how deep
Was the forgetful kingdom of death.

THE MALDIVE SHARK
Herman Melville

About the Shark, phlegmatical one,
Pale sot of the Maldive sea,
The sleek little pilot-fish, azure and slim,
How alert in attendance be.
From his saw-pit of mouth, from his charnel of maw
They have nothing of harm to dread,
But liquidly glide on his ghastly flank
Or before his Gorgonian head;
Or lurk in the port of serrated teeth
In white triple tiers of glittering gates,
And there find a haven where peril's abroad,
An asylum in jaws of the Fates!
They are friends; and friendly they guide him to prey,
Yet never partake of the treat—
Eyes and brains to the dotard lethargic and dull,
Pale ravener of horrible meat.

TERRORS OF THE DEEP

The sea has long drawn poets, who fish in it for images to explain their world. The pilot-fish may have reminded Herman Melville of human parasites. In the following poem, William Carlos Williams is suddenly more frightened by the image of technology, skill, power, and privilege built on centuries of human suffering, than by the wild ocean.

TREACHEROUS NATURE

Read Melville's poem aloud as you might read a children's poem—the singsong rhythm and strong rhyme make an ironic counterpoint to the disturbing images.

Phlegmatical = sluggish.
Sot = drunk.
Gorgonian = monstrous.

THE YACHTS
William Carlos Williams

Contend in a sea which the land partly encloses
shielding them from the too-heavy blows
of an ungoverned ocean which when it chooses

tortures the biggest hulls, the best man knows
to pit against its beatings, and sinks them pitilessly.
Mothlike in mists, scintillant in the minute

brilliance of cloudless days, with broad bellying sails
they glide to the wind tossing green water
from their sharp prows while over them the crew crawls

ant-like, solicitously grooming them, releasing,
making fast as they turn, lean far over and having
caught the wind again, side by side, head for the mark.

In a well guarded arena of open water surrounded by
lesser and greater craft which, sycophant, lumbering
and flittering follow them, they appear youthful, rare

as the light of a happy eye, live with the grace
of all that in the mind is fleckless, free and
naturally to be desired. Now the sea which holds them

is moody, lapping their glossy sides, as if feeling
for some slightest flaw but fails completely.
Today no race. Then the wind comes again. The yachts

move, jockeying for a start, the signal is set and they
are off. Now the waves strike at them but they are too
well made, they slip through, though they take in canvas.

Arms with hands grasping seek to clutch at the prows.
Bodies thrown recklessly in the way are cut aside.
It is a sea of faces about them in agony, in despair

until the horror of the race dawns staggering the mind,
the whole sea become an entanglement of watery bodies
lost to the world bearing what they cannot hold. Broken,

beaten, desolate, reaching from the dead to be taken up
they cry out, failing, failing! their cries rising
in waves still as the skillful yachts pass over.

To the wind = though sail-
boats can't sail directly
into a blowing wind, they
can zigzag, or "tack," in the
general direction.
Mark = the buoy or marker
that racing boats must pass
to begin the race.
Sycophant = fawning and
subservient; major races
are attended by scores of
pleasure boats, watching
the race from a safe
distance.
Signal = yacht races gener-
ally start with the firing
of a cannon or the hoisting
of a flag.
Take in canvas = when the
wind is too strong, boats
reduce the surface area of
their sails, making it more
difficult for strong winds to
knock them over or cause
damage.

VI.

POEMS OF ALIENATION

SUMMER IS ICUMEN IN
Anonymous

THE ENGLISH WEATHER—TWO VARIATIONS

Ezra Pound came across this Middle English poem as a young man, at a time when he was reading medieval languages and translating old poetry into modern verse. Estranged from the moribund poetic scene back in America, and stuck in a grim English winter, he has some grumpy fun at the expense of the "ancient music."

Is icumen = has come; or "is a-coming."
Lhude = loud.
Mead = meadow.
Cu = cow.
Nu = now.
Starteth = startles.
Verteth = this may mean either "leaps" or "farts"— scholars disagree on which.
Ne swik thou = may you never stop.

Summer is icumen in!
Lhudé sing, cuckoo!
Groweth seed and bloweth mead,
And springth the woodé nu.
Sing, cuckoo!

Ewé bleateth after lamb
Lowth after calfé cu.
Bullock starteth, bucké verteth.
Merry sing, cuckoo!
Cuckoo! Cuckoo!
Well singés thou, cuckoo.
Ne swik thou never nu.

refrain

Sing cuckoo nu! Sing cuckoo!
Sing cuckoo nu! Sing cuckoo!

ANCIENT MUSIC
Ezra Pound

Winter is icummen in,
　　Lhude sing Goddamm,
　　Raineth drop and staineth slop,
And how the wind doth ramm!
　　　　Sing: Goddamm.
Skiddeth bus and sloppeth us,
An ague hath my ham.
Freezeth river, turneth liver,
　　　　Damn you, sing: Goddamm.
Goddamm, Goddamm, 'tis why I am, Goddamm,
　　　So 'gainst the winter's balm.
Sing goddamm, damm, sing Goddamm,
Sing goddamm, sing goddamm, DAMM.

NOTE—This is not folk music, but Dr. Ker writes that the tune is to be found under the Latin words of a very ancient canon.

THE CUCKOO'S SONG

Here's another Middle English song to spring, like Chaucer's. It's a true lyric, words for the music of an ancient *rota*, a *canon* or *round* for six voices (much like "Row, Row, Row Your Boat").

POUND AND POETICISMS

Ezra Pound hated the way that poets—particularly modern poets, who ought to know better—insisted on poetic-sounding Middle English *-eth* endings such as "raineth," "hath," and "doth." Pound's not making fun of the original poem, but of those who would translate it in a falsely archaic way. Pound's note tweaks the nineteenth century fad of going to the country to record folk poems and songs. Dr. Ker was an eminent scholar of medieval literature.

It doesn't take much for poets, self-absorbed in the best of situations, to drift into isolation and alienation. Claude McKay adds the further estrangement of race to the mix, and sets his poem in a vast city. Unlike McKay, Native American poet Wendy Rose has brought with her such a powerful sense of connection to her culture that the very landscape begins to change.

THE WHITE CITY
Claude McKay

I will not toy with it nor bend an inch.
Deep in the secret chambers of my heart
I muse my life-long hate, and without flinch
I bear it nobly as I live my part.
My being would be a skeleton, a shell,
If this dark Passion that fills my every mood,
And makes my heaven in the white world's hell,
Did not forever feed me vital blood.
I see the mighty city through a mist—
The strident trains that speed the goaded mass,
The poles and spires and towers vapor-kissed,
The fortressed port through which the great ships pass,
The tides, the wharves, the dens I contemplate,
Are sweet like wanton loves because I hate.

Leaving Port Authority for the St. Regis Rezz
Wendy Rose

I saw a mesa
between two buildings,
a row of tall
thin houses on top
bare like the desert I know,
the roofs occurring
in clumps like greasewood. O Wendy, he said,
looking at his fingernails,
that's Weehawken.

Well
one way or another
we'll get some
where soon
for I have seen crow
dancing on the snow,
a hawk on Henry Street,
smoke plumes on the lips
of streetkids,
mesas
along the Hudson.
I am getting ready.

A HATE SONNET
McKay's poem seems to echo the idea attributed to Nietzsche, "Whatever doesn't kill me, makes me stronger." It's a hate song, not a love song—a sonnet that should be read with bitterness and irony.

Goaded mass = the first commuter trains and subways started running early in the century, creating a new phenomenon: the harried crowd commuting to work.

WEST OF THE HUDSON
New York City's Port Authority Bus Terminal, on the east bank of the Hudson River across from Weehawken, New Jersey, is the nation's busiest and is surrounded by urban decay. The St. Regis Indian Reservation is on the border between upstate New York and Quebec. In any case, the poet is a long way from home.

James Weldon Johnson exalts the unknown authors of African-American spiritual songs as a way of answering the estrangement he feels so keenly.

The sentiment of his tribute may seem slightly dated now, but the unknown singers become a powerful image that stands for the poet's hopes. Johnson employs the same cadence and language of religious oratory that Martin Luther King, Jr., would later employ to such dynamic effect when speaking for the civil rights movement of the 1950s and 1960s.

O BLACK AND UNKNOWN BARDS
James Weldon Johnson

O black and unknown bards of long ago,
How came your lips to touch the sacred fire?
How, in your darkness, did you come to know
The power and beauty of the minstrel's lyre?
Who first from midst his bonds lifted his eyes?
Who first from out the still watch, lone and long,
Feeling the ancient faith of prophets rise
Within his dark-kept soul, burst into song?

Heart of what slave poured out such melody
As "Steal away to Jesus"? On its strains
His spirit must have nightly floated free,
Though still about his hands he felt his chains.
Who heard great "Jordan roll"? Whose starward eye
Saw chariot "swing low"? And who was he
That breathed that comforting, melodic sigh,
"Nobody Knows de Trouble I See"?

What merely living clod, what captive thing,
Could up toward God through all its darkness grope,

And find within its deadened heart to sing

These songs of sorrow, love and faith, and hope?

How did it catch that subtle undertone,

That note in music heard not with the ears?

How sound the elusive reed so seldom blown,

Which stirs the soul or melts the heart to tears.

Not that great German master in his dream

Of harmonies that thundered amongst the stars

At the creation, ever heard a theme

Nobler than "Go down, Moses." Mark its bars

How like a mighty trumpet-call they stir

The blood. Such are the notes that men have sung

Going to valorous deeds; such tones there were

That helped make history when Time was young.

There is a wide, wide wonder in it all,

That from degraded rest and servile toil

The fiery spirit of the seer should call

These simple children of the sun and soil.

O black slave singers, gone, forgot, unfamed,

You—you alone, of all the long, long line

Of those who've sung untaught, unknown, unnamed,

Have stretched out upward, seeking the divine.

MUSIC EMPYREAN

Deeply interested in music, Johnson wrote many song lyrics during his varied career as writer, journalist, diplomat, and teacher. In his famous volume *God's Trombones*, he rendered into verse sermons that he recalled from childhood and youth. This poem should be read aloud almost like a sermon, or the singing of a spiritual hymn.

Sacred fire = the universe, as described by Ptolemy, had five heavens, the last of which was pure fire. *Clod* = piece of earth. *German master* = possibly Hayden, composer of "The Creation" oratorio. *Empyrean* = the heaven of fire, in Ptolemy's universe, where the deity was to be found.

You sang not deeds of heroes or of kings;
No chant of bloody war, no exulting paean
Of arms-won triumphs; but your humble strings
You touched in chord with music empyrean.
You sang far better than you knew; the songs
That for your listeners' hungry hearts sufficed
Still live,—but more than this to you belongs:
You sang a race from wood and stone to Christ.

THE HEART
Stephen Crane

In the desert
I saw a creature, naked, bestial
Who, squatting upon the ground,
Held his heart in his hands,
And ate of it.
I said, "Is it good, friend?"
"It is bitter—bitter," he answered;
"But I like it
Because it is bitter,
And because it is my heart."

HEARTS GROWN BRUTAL

A poet, writing about the heart, is not just talking about the beating muscle that drives the vascular system. In these by Steve Crane and Léonie Adams we see two poems about the alienated heart that would hardly do for Valentine's Day.

BECAUSE IT IS BITTER

Is this really a poem? It's unquestionably a powerful image, with tremendous rhetorical force. Crane called his verses "lines," rather than "poems." As is the case with most of his lines, it's a vision, something of a parable, whose lesson is appalling—the human capacity for alienation and self-hate that feeds upon itself and twists the mind.

This poem was written when Adams was still an undergraduate at Barnard College, and despite a few rather conventional phrases it's a powerful, mature work. Like the opening to Eliot's "The Waste Land," it makes use of the *reverdie* tradition to contrast the green of spring with the alienation that the poet feels.

Thou also art = you are also.

APRIL MORTALITY
Léonie Adams

Rebellion shook an ancient dust,
  And bones bleached dry of rottenness
Said Heart, be bitter still, nor trust
  The earth, the sky, in their bright dress.

Heart, heart, dost thou not break to know
  This anguish thou wilt bear alone?
We sang of it an age ago,
  And traced it dimly upon stone.

With all the drifting race of men
  Thou also art begot to mourn
That she is crucified again,
  The lonely Beauty yet unborn.

And if thou dreamest to have won
  Some touch of her in permanence,
'Tis the old cheating of the sun,
  The intricate lovely play of sense.

Be bitter still, remember how
  Four petals, when a little breath
Of wind made stir the pear-tree bough,
  Blew delicately down to death.

LAST RESPECTS

Both speakers in the poems by Christina Rossetti and Alberto Ríos seem objective—without an axe to grind. But there's a clear ironic message to both poems, and no doubt that the poets' real subjects are passion, estrangement, blame, and guilt.

AFTER DEATH
Christina Rossetti

The curtains were half drawn; the floor was swept
  And strewn with rushes; rosemary and may
    Lay thick upon the bed on which I lay,
Where, through the lattice, ivy-shadows crept.
He leaned above me, thinking that I slept
  And could not hear him; but I heard him say,
    "Poor child, poor child"; and as he turned away
Came a deep silence, and I knew he wept.
He did not touch the shroud, or raise the fold
  That hid my face, or take my hand in his,
    Or ruffle the smooth pillows for my head.
    He did not love me living; but once dead
He pitied me; and very sweet it is
To know he still is warm though I am cold.

True Story of the Pins
Alberto Ríos

Pins are always plentiful
but one day they were not
and your Uncle Humberto
who collected all the butterflies
you see here on the walls,
was crazy looking for some
and he went to your cousin
Graciela the hard seamstress
who has pins it is rumored
even in hard times
but when she found out
why he wanted them
because the wind was from the south
who was her friend
since the days of her
childhood on the sea
told her, she firmly refused
your poor Uncle Humberto
whose picture is here
on the wall behind you,

Cold Comfort
As in "The Unquiet Grave," Rossetti's is told by a voice from beyond. But Rossetti's main device here is irony: even the sonnet form itself makes a comment about the lack of love in this relationship. Notice how separating rhymes by many lines mutes their effect, and how Rossetti ends the poem with a whisper, rather than the bang you expect from a sonnet.

A Family Quarrel
Poets often employ the voice of a speaker who doesn't understand the significance of everything he's saying. Read Ríos's poem as if you were telling a story about your own family to someone you knew. Notice how intense details are expressed almost as afterthoughts—particularly the eyes of the picture of Uncle Humberto, and the description of the vein on his forehead.

did you feel his eyes,
and he went into the most terrible
of rages, too terrible
for a butterfly collector
we all said afterward
and he burst the vein
that grew like a great snake
on his small forehead
and he died on the dirt
floor of Graciela's house
who of course felt sick
and immediately went
and put pins, this is what has
made her hard, through
the bright wings of the butterflies
Humberto had prepared
since he was after all
her father and she
could afford no better
light of perpetuity.

DELIGHT IN DISORDER
Robert Herrick

A sweet disorder in the dress
Kindles in clothes a wantonness:
A lawn about the shoulders thrown
Into a fine distraction:
An erring lace, which here and there
Enthralls the crimson stomacher:
A cuff neglectful, and thereby
Ribbands to flow confusèdly
A winning wave (deserving note)
In the tempestuous petticoat:
A careless shoestring, in whose tie
I see a wild civility:
Do more bewitch me than when art
Is too precise in every part.

DRESS CODES

Poetic fashions change
much as dress fashions
do. Modern poets helped
revive the once-unfashion-
able "rough" verse, vivid
imagery, and outrageous
subjects of the so-called
"Metaphysical Poets" of
the mid-1600s, including
Herrick, Donne, and
Marvell. But as the century
draws to a close, and (as
Lynne McMahon suggests
in the following poem)
sexuality seems more
frightening and dangerous
again, restraint and form in
verse may soon be back in
fashion too.

Lawn = scarf.
Stomacher = a part of the
bodice, held in place by
laces.
Ribbands = ribbons.
Art = also carries the sense
of *artifice*.

DEVOLUTION OF THE NUDE
Lynne McMahon

In Whitman's day there were the secret bathers
spied on by his poem's spinster, yearning
behind the glass; in Emerson's day
and Thoreau's; in the Utopian societies eager
to transmute the dross of Puritanism into the gold
of burnished flesh; in every century or half-
century there have been faddists who know
the six openings of the body must go
unstoppered, that the distinction between man
and woman is holy, and the expulsion from
the garden was the garment district's
first advertisement ploy.

                    In our day
there are perhaps fewer of these: acid rain
and factory seepage combine to forecast another
ice-age (this time the glacier greens with alloys),
have made stoppering hygienic;
and we've discovered in place of the open,
the principle of the closed, the Victorian tenet

that covered is more alluring than bare,
that Shame's the secret passageway
to Eros. And though we may laugh at Marianne
Moore's remark—"I like the nude," she said,
handing back Kenneth Clark's book, "but
in moderation"—it is us

        we find
swathed in bedclothes, as if we were asthmatic
invalids under covers, calming ourselves
with penlights and turn-of-the-century novels
whose characters' cumbersome cloaks
and flannel layers protect them, protect us,
from what is only whispered of: the difficult
birth in the back room, the laying out
of the dead in the parlor, the two occasions
for nakedness that are dreadful
and not for our eyes—

        not yet.

SECRET BATHERS

In Walt Whitman's long poem, "Song of Myself," a famous passage describes a group of men skinny-dipping in the surf, and a woman watching them from her window, imagining that she's frolicking with them. Sir Kenneth Clark was an English art historian. His *Civilization* and numerous other books on Renaissance, Baroque, and Romantic painting, were often lavishly illustrated with nudes. Read this one aloud as if you were talking with someone about what to wear—a lighthearted conversation that leads to a disturbing realization.

OF THEE I SING

Maybe it's unfair to hold poems that belong to an earlier era to today's standards of political correctness. When it was written, for instance, Stephen Vincent Benét's poem must have seemed an affectionate celebration of America's rough edges. Now, though, it seems full of ironies—a poem about America that leaves many Americans completely out. In the poem that follows it, the recent Nobel laureate Derek Walcott, a black West Indian who teaches poetry in New England, shows a different understanding of the harsh realities on which the American myth was built.

AMERICAN NAMES
Stephen Vincent Benét

I have fallen in love with American names,
The sharp names that never get fat,
The snakeskin-titles of mining-claims,
The plumed war-bonnet of Medicine Hat,
Tucson and Deadwood and Lost Mule flat.

Seine and Piave are silver spoons,
But the spoonbowl-metal is thin and worn,
There are English counties like hunting-tunes
Played on keys of a postboy's horn,
But I will remember where I was born.

I will remember Carquinez Straits,
Little French Lick and Lundy's Lane,
The Yankee ships and the Yankee dates
And the bullet-towns of Calamity Jane.
I will remember Skunktown Plain.

I will fall in love with a Salem tree
And a rawhide quirt from Santa Cruz,

I will get me a bottle of Boston sea
And a blue-gum nigger to sing me blues.
I am tired of loving a foreign muse.

Rue des Martyrs and Bleeding-Heart-Yard,
Senlis, Pisa, and Blindman's Oast,
It is a magic ghost you guard
But I am sick for a newer ghost,
Harrisburg, Spartanburg, Painted Post.

Henry and John were never so
And Henry and John were always right?
Granted, but when it was time to go
And the tea and the laurels had stood all night,
Did they never watch for Nantucket Light?

I shall not rest quiet in Montparnasse.
I shall not lie easy in Winchelsea.
You may bury my body in Sussex grass,
You may bury my tongue at Champmédy.
I shall not be there. I shall rise and pass.
Bury my heart at Wounded Knee.

Old New England
Derek Walcott

Rocket = skyrockets were sometimes used to signal the arrival of sailing ships.
Iroquois = American Indians displaced by the settlement of New England.
Spring = season; water source.
Lance = weapon; surgical procedure.
Shroud = line supporting a ship's mast; a burial garment.
Crosstrees = ship's masts and booms; steeples.

Black clippers, tarred with whales' blood, fold their sails
entering New Bedford, New London, New Haven.
A white church spire whistles into space
like a swordfish, a rocket pierces heaven
as the thawed springs in icy chevrons race
down hillsides and Old Glories flail
the crosses of green farm boys back from 'Nam.
Seasons are measured still by the same
span of the veined leaf and the veined body
whenever the spring wind startles an uproar
of marching oaks with memories of a war
that peeled whole counties from the calendar.

The hillside is still wounded by the spire
of the white meetinghouse, the Indian trail
trickles down it like the brown blood of the whale
in rowanberries bubbling like the spoor
on logs burnt black as Bibles by hellfire.
The war whoop is coiled tight in the white owl,

stone-feathered icon of the Indian soul,
and railway lines are arrowing to the far
mountainwide absence of the Iroquois.
Spring lances wood and wound, and a spring runs
down tilted birch floors with their splintered suns
of beads and mirrors—broken promises
that helped make this Republic what it is.

The crest of our conviction grows as loud
as the spring oaks, rooted and reassured
that God is meek but keeps a whistling sword;
His harpoon is the white lance of the church,
His wandering mind a trail folded in birch,
His rage the vats that boiled the melted beast
when the black clippers brought (knotting each shroud
round the crosstrees) our sons home from the East.

DOUBLE TALK

Here's a poem about
multiple meanings. The
landscape has two mean-
ings, as do many of the
words. Past and present
come together for Walcott.
For example, the last line
brings to mind not only the
Vietnam War dead, but
the New England whale
trade that replaced traffic
in slaves in the 1800s.
Read this one slowly so
you don't miss the play of
sound and sense. The
words connect quite subtly
for example, the "rocket"
and "Old Glories" may
conjure up an echo of
our national anthem. Go
too fast and you'll miss
Walcott's careful allitera-
tion (*war whoop/white*)
and unobtrusive rhyme.

TWO HOMELANDS

Here are two final poems of alienation. One sounds a note of hope for the future, of a long, dark road's end suddenly in sight. The other is a song of despair and loss. The American-born Karl Shapiro, separated by an ocean from the newly created Israel, finds himself somehow able to live in America more easily knowing that the Jewish homeland exists at last. For the Palestinian poet Fadwa Tuqan, the exhausting prospect of a life adrift is suddenly terribly real, terribly frightening.

ISRAEL
Karl Shapiro

When I think of the liberation of Palestine,
When my eye conceives the great black English line
Spanning the world news of two thousand years,
My heart leaps forward like a hungry dog,
My heart is thrown back on its tangled chain,
My soul is hangdog in a Western chair.

When I think of the battle for Zion I hear
The drop of chains, the starting forth of feet
And I remain chained in a Western chair.
My blood beats like a bird against a wall,
I feel the weight of prisons in my skull
Falling away; my forbears stare through stone.

When I see the name of Israel high in print
The fences crumble in my flesh; I sink
Deep in a Western chair and rest my soul.
I look the stranger clear to the blue depths
Of his unclouded eye. I say my name
Aloud for the first time unconsciously.

Speak of the tillage of a million heads
No more. Speak of the evil myth no more
Of one who harried Jesus on his way
Saying, Go faster. Speak no more
Of the yellow badge, secta nefaria.
Speak the name only of the living land.

HOMECOMING

Shapiro's poem was inspired by the 1948 United Nations partition of Palestine and the subsequent Arab-Israeli war that marked the beginning of the modern Israel. It is written from the point of view of an American looking on from a distance, but who, despite that distance, sees in the founding of Israel the end of two millennia of exile.

Tillage = the mass slaughter of Jews by the Nazis.
Yellow badge = Jews, in Germany and elsewhere, were often forced to wear yellow badges.
Secta nefaria = the people of evil, a name sometimes used to justify anti-Semitism.
Living land = Israel as a country, rather than as a race.

THE LAST KNOCKS
Fadwa Tuqan (translated by Issa J. Boullata)

Will You not open this door for me
My hand is exhausted of knocking, knocking at Your door
I have come to Your vastness to beg
Some tranquility
And peace of mind
But Your vastness is closed
In my face, drowned in silence
O Lord of the house
The door was open here
The house was the refuge of all burdened with grief
The door was open here
And the green olive tree rose high
Embracing the house
The oil lighting without fire
Guiding the steps of him who walks at night
Giving relief to the one crushed by the burden of the
Earth
flooding him with satisfaction and tranquility
Do You hear me O Lord of the house
After my loss in the deserts

Away from You I have returned to You

But Your vastness is closed

In my face, drowned in silence

Your vastness is shrouded

With the dust of death

If You are here open the door for me

Do not veil Your face from me

See my orphanhood, my loss

Amid the ruins of my collapsing world

The grief of the Earth on my shoulders

And the terrors of a tyrant destiny

VII.

ART, POETRY, AND THE MAKING THEREOF

GROWING THINGS
AND DYING THINGS

As you might guess,
poets love to write about
the writing of poetry.
Sometimes this subject
shows up artfully dis-
guised. Here Philip Larkin
seems to be writing about
trees, and Sylvia Plath's
apparent subject is a lane
winding through a thicket
of blackberries. But Larkin
sees in the trees something
of his own struggle to keep
writing in the face of
growing older. For Plath,
who ended up killing her-
self, no such message is
to be found: all the life
around her is corrupt and
dying, and at the end of the
road she finds emptiness.

THE TREES
Philip Larkin

The trees are coming into leaf
Like something almost being said;
The recent buds relax and spread,
Their greenness is a kind of grief.

Is it that they are born again
And we grow old? No, they die too.
Their yearly trick of looking new
Is written down in rings of grain.

Yet still the unresting castles thresh
In fullgrown thickness every May.
Last year is dead, they seem to say,
Begin afresh, afresh, afresh.

BLACKBERRYING
Sylvia Plath

Nobody in the lane, and nothing, nothing but
blackberries,
Blackberries on either side, though on the right mainly,
A blackberry alley, going down in hooks, and a sea
Somewhere at the end of it, heaving. Blackberries
Big as the ball of my thumb, and dumb as eyes
Ebon in the hedges, fat
With blue-red juices. These they squander on my fingers.
I had not asked for such a blood sisterhood; they must
love me.
They accommodate themselves to my milkbottle,
flattening their sides.

Overhead go the choughs in black, cacophonous flocks—
Bits of burnt paper wheeling in a blown sky.
Theirs is the only voice, protesting, protesting.
I do not think the sea will appear at all.
The high, green meadows are glowing, as if lit from
within.
I come to one bush of berries so ripe it is a bush of flies,

LEAVES

Larkin's exquisite poems
are often about failure
or inadequacy. Here he
finds in the trees an exam-
ple that helps him keep
writing. In the last stanza,
Larkin uses words that
sound like branches rustling
in the breeze. The last line
should whisper like the
wind.

BRIARS

Gathering berries and
nuts ("berrying" and
"nutting") are traditional
English country pastimes.
Don't read this one before
putting berries on your
morning cereal, though—
here the poet finds them
bursting with sick, corrupt,
consuming life. She is
much happier with
emptiness.

Choughs = the common
name for several species of
crowlike birds found in
England.

Hanging their bluegreen bellies and their wing panes in a
    Chinese screen.
The honey-feast of the berries has stunned them; they
    believe in heaven.
One more hook, and the berries and bushes end.

The only thing to come now is the sea.
From between two hills a sudden wind funnels at me,
Slapping its phantom laundry in my face.
These hills are too green and sweet to have tasted salt.
I follow the sheep path between them. A last hook brings
    me
To the hills' northern face, and the face is orange rock
That looks out on nothing, nothing but a great space
Of white and pewter lights, and a din like silversmiths
Beating and beating at an intractable metal.

COON SONG
A. R. Ammons

I got one good look
   in the raccoon's eyes
      when he fell from the tree
came to his feet
   and perfectly still
      seized the baying hounds
in his dull fierce stare,
   in that recognition all
      decision lost,
choice irrelevant, before the
   battle fell
      and the unwinding
of his little knot of time began:

   Dostoevsky would think
it important if the coon
   could choose to
      be back up the tree:
or if he could choose to be
   wagging by a swamp pond

THE POET IS A LONELY HUNTER

As we've seen, poets sometimes put on the guise of storytellers. Here, though, A. R. Ammons has some fun with it—making us pay attention to our own expectations as we read his story, to our own wish for happy endings, to our own desire for a satisfying beginning, middle, and end. But soon after he begins telling his story the order begins dissolving, the artificiality of the story is made apparent, the poet's game-playing takes over, and all that is left at the end is the poet and his reader or listener.

THE GAME

In this poem we start out on a coon hunt and end up on a wild-goose chase. Coon hunting is a traditional pastime in the American South, from which Ammons hails. Coon dogs chase a raccoon until they tree it, and it can be shot or knocked from the tree by the hunter, for the dogs to finish off. It's done for the excitement and the sport of watching the dogs dispatch the coon, rather than for food. Reading this out loud can be a lot of fun, particularly in front of an audience. It starts off as if it's telling a story. Then, just as it gets to the exciting part, the kill, it becomes clear how the poet is teasing, manipulating his audience—he's more interested in counting spaces.

dabbling at scuttling
crawdads the coon may have
      dreamed in fact of curling
         into the holed-out gall
of a fallen oak some squirrel
      had once brought
         high into the air
clean leaves to but

      reality can go to hell
is what the coon's eyes said to me:
      and said how simple
         the solution to my
problem is: it needs only
      not to be I thought the raccoon
         felt no anger,
saw none; cared nothing for cowardice,
      bravery; was in fact
         bored at
knowing what would ensue:
      the unwinding, the whirling growls,
         exposed tenders,
the wet teeth—a problem to be
      solved, the taut-coiled vigor

of the hunt
ready to snap loose:

    you want to know what happened,
you want to hear me describe it,
    to placate the hound's-mouth
      slobbering in your own heart
I will not tell you: actually the coon
    possessing secret knowledge
      pawed dust on the dogs
and they disappeared, yapping into
    nothingness, and the coon went
      down to the pond
and washed his face and hands and beheld
    the world: maybe he didn't:
      I am no slave that I
should entertain you, say what you want
    to hear, let you wallow in
      your silt: one two three four five:
one two three four five six seven eight nine ten:

    (all this time I've been
      counting spaces
while you were thinking of something else)

Count those spaces slowly, deliberately, while your audience wonders what's going on. It's a game, as the "here-we-go-round" section indicates. You could even sing those words to the tune of "Here-We-Go-Round the Mulberry Bush." The poet is going around and around the story. In the end, like Wallace Stevens in "The Emperor of Ice Cream," he chooses between seeming (the story of the coon) and being (the reality of the poet talking to his audience).

mess in your own sloppy silt:
the hounds disappeared
yelping (the way you would at extinction)
into——the order
breaks up here——immortality:
I know that's where you think the brave
little victims should go:
I do not care what
you think I do not care what you think:
I do not care what you
think: one two three four five
six seven eight nine ten here we go
round the here-we-go-round, the
here-we-go round, the here-we-
go-round: coon will end in disorder at the
teeth of hounds: the situation
will get him:
spheres roll, cubes stay put: now there
one two three four five
are two philosophies:
here we go round the mouth-wet of hounds:

what I choose
is youse:
baby

From The Prologue

Anne Bradstreet

I am obnoxious to each carping tongue
Who says my hand a needle better fits.
A poet's pen all scorn I should thus wrong;
For such despite they cast on female wits,
If what I do prove well, it won't advance—
They'll say it's stolen, or else it was by chance.

But sure the antique Greeks were far more mild,
Else of our sex why feignéd they those Nine,
and Poesy made Calliope's own child?
So 'mongst the rest they placed the Arts Divine.
But this weak knot they will full soon untie—
The Greeks did nought but play the fools and lie.

Let Greeks be Greeks, and women what they are.
Men have precedency, and still excel.
It is but vain unjustly to wage war.
Men can do best, and women know it well.
Preëminence in all and each is yours—
Yet grant some small acknowledgment of ours.

LOST VOICES

Many uncelebrated writers have produced notable poetry. But, as they didn't belong to mainstream literary circles, they were soon forgotten. Today, scholars are discovering what such voices say about their world, and redefining literary merit. Here, early American poet Anne Bradstreet chafes at the reception she knows her poems will receive. Gwendolyn Brooks, herself an honored American poet, knows that the pool players she writes about here will leave nothing behind unless she gives them voices.

Nine = the muses, from which comes inspiration.
Calliope = preeminent among the nine muses, inspiration for epic and heroic poems.

EACH CARPING TONGUE

Bradstreet emigrated to America in the mid-1600s. Practical skills were what counted there, and she despaired that her voice would be heard. Her poems were published in England without her consent during her lifetime, but more as a literary curiosity than anything else.

Thyme or parsley / bays = a wreath of laurel, or bay laurel, was worn by Roman poets; it is also a cooking herb; thyme and parsley are common cooking herbs more "fitting" for a woman.

And oh, ye high flown quills that soar the skies,

And ever with your prey still catch your praise,

If e'er you deign these lowly lines your eyes,

Give thyme or parsley wreath; I ask no bays.

This mean and unrefinéd ore of mine

Will make your glistering gold but more to shine.

WE REAL COOL
Gwendolyn Brooks

The Pool Players. Seven at the Golden Shovel.

We real cool. We
Left school. We

Lurk late. We
Strike straight. We

Sing sin. We
Thin gin. We

Jazz June. We
Die soon.

PRIDE AND DESPAIR

Brooks's poems often give voice to the voiceless, and feature speakers from the inner city caught in hopeless situations. Here, in a handful of monosyllabic couplets, the pool players convey the pride and inarticulate despair by which so many in this environment live their lives. Brooks wrote the poem in the 1950s, but it anticipates the sort of street poetry that would show up in rap music thirty years later.

THE PLASTIC ARTS

Every picture tells a story, they say, and sometimes work in the "plastic" arts— those arts having to do with form and shape— finds its way into poetry. It's a good way of talking about the art of poetry without quite saying so. Siegfried Sassoon, unhappy with ill-informed museum-goers, knows that the same audience exists for literature. X. J. Kennedy, on the other hand, seems to sympathize with the struggling patrons.

IN THE NATIONAL GALLERY
Siegfried Sassoon

Faces irresolute and unperplexed,—

Unspeculative faces, bored and weak,

Cruise past each patient victory of technique

Dimly desiring to enjoy the next

Yet never finding what they seem to seek.

Here blooms, recedes, and glows before their eyes

A quintessential world preserved in paint,

Calm vistas of long-vanished Paradise,

And ripe remembrances of sage and saint;

The immortality of changeless skies,

And all bright legendries of Time's creation . . .

    Yet I observe no gestures of surprise

    From those who straggle in to patronize

    The Art Collection of the English Nation.

NUDE DESCENDING A STAIRCASE
X. J. Kennedy

Toe upon toe, a snowing flesh,
A gold of lemon, root and rind,
She sifts in sunlight down the stairs
With nothing on. Nor on her mind.

We spy beneath the banister.
A constant thresh of thigh on thigh—
Her lips imprint the swinging air
That parts to let her parts go by.

One-woman waterfall, she wears
Her slow descent like a long cape
And pausing, on the final stair
Collects her motions into shape.

PATRONIZING BEAUTY

Sassoon went through a shattering war experience in World War I and developed a grudge against the populace the war was fought for—a populace he found so often indifferent and oblivious to what was going on.

STOP-ACTION

"Nude Descending a Staircase" (1912) is the best-known painting by Marcel Duchamp. Painted during the height of the Cubist and Futurist periods of modern art, it resembles a stop-action photo sequence. Here Kennedy—best known for verse that doesn't take itself too seriously—puts himself in the shoes of a museum-goer and pays playful tribute to a painting that almost everybody knows.

SONNET—TO SCIENCE
Edgar Allan Poe

FACT AND ABSTRACT

How can you write a decent poem about the nature of the universe when its nature changes with each new scientific theory? That seems to be the question Edgar Allan Poe asks. For Wallace Stevens, that's not a problem. In fact, he suggests, there's far more wonder in what *is* than in what *seems to be.*

Diana = Roman goddess of the moon.
Car = chariot, carriage.
Hamadryad = tree nymph.
Naiad = water nymph.

IN PRAISE OF LOW-TECH

Poe's complaint here is that all we are left with is scientific fact. When will it return to the way it was? Nevermore.

Science! true daughter of Old Time thou art!
  Who alterest all things with thy peering eyes.
Why preyest thou thus upon the poet's heart,
  Vulture, whose wings are dull realities?
How should he love thee? or how deem thee wise,
  Who wouldst not leave him in his wandering
To seek for treasure in the jewelled skies,
  Albeit he soared with an undaunted wing?
Hast thou not dragged Diana from her car?
  And driven the Hamadryad from the wood
To seek a shelter in some happier star?
  Hast thou not torn the Naiad from her flood,
The Elfin from the green grass, and from me
The summer dream beneath the tamarind tree?

THE EMPEROR OF ICE-CREAM
Wallace Stevens

Call the roller of big cigars,
The muscular one, and bid him whip
In kitchen cups concupiscent curds.
Let the wenches dawdle in such dress
As they are used to wear, and let the boys
Bring flowers in last month's newspapers.
Let be be finale of seem.
The only emperor is the emperor of ice-cream.

Take from the dresser of deal,
Lacking the three glass knobs, that sheet
On which she embroidered fantails once
And spread it so as to cover her face.
If her horny feet protrude, they come
To show how cold she is, and dumb.
Let the lamp affix its beam.
The only emperor is the emperor of ice-cream.

CONCUPISCENT CURDS

A lot of people read this famous poem, understanding every word, and then ask, "Huh?" Don't let it confuse you. Stevens's theory of poetry was "no ideas but in things." So when Stevens writes of "big cigars," an obvious Freudian symbol, he's saying, "No. It's just a cigar unless you make it otherwise." This poem is full of outrageous puns, suggestive language, and obvious symbols. Forget all that, the poet says. Ice cream—delicious and tempting—is an absolute good, and not a symbol for anything. The way words sound here is as important as what they mean. You should have fun with words like "concupiscent," "wenches," "dawdle," "horny," and so forth.

Concupiscent = seductive.
Finale = the end.
Deal = planks of fir or pine.

RUM, RAM, RUF

One of the characters in Chaucer's *Canterbury Tales* scoffs at old-fashioned alliterative verse, claiming that he can't "geste Rum-Ram-Ruf by lettre." This ancient form of poetry out loud dates back centuries before English was a written language. Here, Fred Chappell, using modern English, turns to the way English poetry was recited in the days of the Anglo-Saxons, when the language was perhaps closer to German than to modern English.

MY GRANDFATHER'S CHURCH GOES UP

Fred Chappell

(Acts 2 1–47)

God is a fire in the head.—*Nijinsky*

Holocaust, pentecost   what heaped heartbreak

The tendrils of fire   forthrightly tasting
foundation to rooftree   flesh of that edifice . . .
Why was sear sent   to sunder those jointures,
the wheat-hued wood   wasted to heaven?
Both alter and apse   the air ascended
in sullen smoke.

    (It was surely no sign
of God's salt grievance   but grizzled Weird grimly
and widely wandering.)

    The dutiful worshipers
stood afar ghast-struck   as the green cedar shingles
burst outward like birds   disturbed in their birling.
Choir stall crushed inward   flayed planking in curlicues
back on it bending,   broad beams of chestnut
oak poplar and pine   gasht open paint-pockets.

And the organ uttered   an unholy Omega
as gilt pipes and pedals   pulsed into rubble.

How it all took tongue!   A total hosannah
this building burgeoned,   the black hymnals whispering
leaves lisping in agony   leaping alight,
sopranos' white scapulars   each singly singeing
robes of the baritones   roaring like rivers
the balcony bellowing   and buckling. In the basement
where the M.Y.F.   had mumbled for mercies
the cane-bottomed chairs   chirruped Chinese.
What a glare   of garish glottals
rose from the nave   what knar-mouth natter!
And the transept tottered   intoning like tympani
as the harsh heat   held hold there.
The whole church resounded   reared its rare anthem
crying out Christ-mercy   to the cloud-cloven sky.

Those portents Saint Paul   foretold to us peoples
fresh now appeared   bifurcate fire-tongues,
and as of wild winds   a swart mighty wrestling,
blood fire and vapor   of smoke vastly vaulting,
the sun into darkness   deadened and dimmed,
wonders in heaven   signs wrought in the world:

Old English poems often used a device called a *kenning*—a concrete image that conveys an abstract meaning. Here, Chappell imitates this with phrases such as "mind-gripped," when he could have said "understood." This sort of poem has a bounding, percussive rhythm. In general, each half-line has two beats, with the alliterating words stressed "force of the fire [slight pause] felt furiously." The trick is to do this without turning it into a singsong, keeping the sense of the sentences intact.

the Spirit poured out   on souls of us sinners.
In this din as of drunkenness   the old men dreamed
    dreams,
the daughters and sons   supernal sights saw.
God's gaudy grace   grasped them up groaning.
Doubt parched within them   pure power overtaking
their senses. Sobbing   like sweethearts bereft
the brothers and sisters   burst into singing.
Truly the Holy   Ghost here now halted,
held sway in their hearts   healed there the hurt.

Now over the narthex   the neat little steeple
force of the fire   felt furiously.
Bruit of black smoke   borne skyward
shadowed its shutters   swam forth in swelter.
It stood as stone   for onstreaming moments
then carefully crumpled   closed inward in char.
The brass bell within it   broke loose, bountifully
pealing, plunged   plangent to the pavement
and a glamour of clangor   gored cloudward gaily.

That was the ringing that wrung   remorse out of us clean,
the elemental echo   the elect would hear always;
in peace or in peril   that peal would pull them.

Seventeen seasons   have since parted
the killing by fire   of my grandfather's kirk.
Moving of our Maker   on this middle earth
is not to be mind-gripped   by any men.

Here Susan and I   saw it, come
to this wood, wicker   basket and wool blanket
swung between us,   in sweet June
on picnic. Prattling   like parakeets
we smoothed out for our meal-place   the mild meadow
    grasses
and spread our sandwiches   in the sunlit greensward.
Then amorously ate.   And afterward
lay languorous and   looking lazily.
Green grass and pokeweed   gooseberry bushes
pink rambling rose   and raspberry vine
sassafras and thistle   and serrate sawbriar
clover and columbine   clung to the remnants,
grew in that ground   once granted to God.
Blackbirds and thrushes   built blithely there
the ferret and kingsnake   fed in the footing.
The wilderness rawly   had walked over those walls
and the deep-drinking forest   driven them down.

Narthex = interior passage of a church.
Clean = entirely.
Vaward = to the front, vanguard.
Chrisom = a ceremonial garment; a sacramental anointing.

Now silence sang: swoon of wind
ambled the oak trees   and arching aspens.

In happy half-sleep   I heard or half-heard
in the bliss of breeze   breath of my grandfather,
vaunt of his voice   advance us vaward.
No fears fretted me   and a freedom followed
this vision vouchsafed,   victory of spirit.
He in the wind   wept not, but wonderfully
spoke softly   soothing to peace.

What mattered he murmured   I never remembered,
words melted in wisps   washed whitely away;
but calm came into me   and cool repose.
Where Fate had fixed   no fervor formed;
he had accepted   wholeness of his handiwork.

gain it was given   to the Grace-grain that grew it,
had gone again   gleaming to Genesis

to the stark beginning   where the first stars burned.
Touchless and tristless   Time took it anew
and changed that church-plot   to an enchanted chrisom
of leaf and flower   of the lithe light and shade.

Pilgrim, the past   becomes prayer
becomes remembrance rock-real   of Resurrection
when the Willer so willeth   works his wild wonders.

THINGS THAT LAST

Poets keep returning to the notion that something, or someone's life, can be captured eternally in poetry. Here, George Herbert seeks to preserve a day, a rose, and a gentle season, in the same breath claiming that only a virtuous soul is immortal. Part of what has made the AIDS epidemic so wrenching is the idea that it's a payback for *sinful* souls, a "divine judgment" against the gay community, where AIDS has hit hardest. Anthony Hecht's wry tribute to poet David Kalstone captures the terrible injustice and irony of it all.

VIRTUE
George Herbert

Sweet day, so cool, so calm, so bright,
The bridal of the earth and sky:
The dew shall weep thy fall tonight;
    For thou must die.

Sweet rose, whose hue angry and brave
Bids the rash gazer wipe his eye:
Thy root is ever in its grave,
    And thou must die.

Sweet spring, full of sweet days and roses,
A box where sweets compacted lie;
My music shows ye have your closes,
    And all must die.

Only a sweet and virtuous soul,
Like seasoned timber, never gives;
But though the whole world turn to coal,
    Then chiefly lives.

IN MEMORY OF DAVID KALSTONE
Who Died of AIDS
Anthony Hecht

Lime-and-mint mayonnaise and salsa verde
Accompanied poached fish that Helen made
For you and J.M. when you came to see us
Just at the salmon season. Now a shade,

A faint blurred absence who before had been
Funny, intelligent, kindness itself,
You leave behind, beside the shock of death,
Three of the finest books upon my shelf.

"Men die from time to time," said Rosalind,
"But not," she said, "for love." A lot she knew!
From the green world of Africa the plague
Wiped out the Forest of Arden, the whole crew

Of innocents, of which, poor generous ghost,
You were among the liveliest. Your friend
Scattered upon the calm Venetian tides
Your sifted ashes so they might descend

A POEM OF DEVOTION
Herbert, who was (as many of the Metaphysical poets were) a cleric, uses the language and imagery of love poetry for a religious subject.

PASTORAL TRAGEDY
Poet David Kalstone's passing seems to leave barely a ripple. Hecht calls to mind Shakespeare's *As You Like It*, where the traditions of pastoral poetry are spoofed when a group of court nobles runs away to live in an innocent, make-believe pastoral paradise in the forest of Arden.

Die = a common Shakespearian pun on sexual climax.
Africa = the virus that causes AIDS is thought to have originated there.
Palazzo Barbaro / Grand Canal = landmarks in Venice.

Even to the bottom of the monstrous world
Or lap at marble steps and pass below
The little bridges, whirl and eddy through
A liquified Palazzo Barbaro.

That mirrored splendor briefly entertains
Your passing as the whole edifice trembles
Within the waters of the Grand Canal,
And writhes and twists, wrinkles and reassembles.

MISSING DATES
William Empson

Slowly the poison the whole blood stream fills.
It is not the effort nor the failure tires.
The waste remains, the waste remains and kills.

It is not your system or clear sight that mills
Down small to the consequence a life requires;
Slowly the poison the whole blood stream fills.

They bled an old dog dry yet the exchange rills
Of young dog blood gave but a month's desires.
The waste remains, the waste remains and kills.

It is the Chinese tombs and the slag hills
Usurp the soil, and not the soil retires.
Slowly the poison the whole blood stream fills.

Not to have fire is to be a skin that shrills.
The complete fire is death. From partial fires
The waste remains, the waste remains and kills.

LOSING BY NUMBERS

Maybe it's no coincidence that these two poems that touch on how hard it is to write are both written in one of the hardest forms to do well, the villanelle. If you compare Bishop's villanelle to Empson's, and to Dylan Thomas's "Do Not Go Gentle into That Good Night," you'll notice that she takes some liberties with the form (actually, so does Empson) —lines an extra beat too long, refrains that don't exactly repeat, and so forth. But the obsessive, repetitive rhyming of the form still drives it. In both Empson's and Bishop's poem, the subject is a repeated behavior—waste, loss—that has a cumulative effect. The villanelle, with its repeated rhymes and refrains, reinforces that effect.

Rills = small streams or rivulets; *exchange rills* has the sense here of "transfusions."

Slag hills = mining waste. *Skin that shrills* = this difficult phrase may mean that without some sort of "fire" inside you—the passions and rages and urges that drive us—life is empty, a skin with no body, and what we say becomes merely shrill noise. But a by-product of fires that don't burn hot enough is the waste that kills.

It is the poems you have lost, the ills
From missing dates, at which the heart expires.
Slowly the poison the whole blood stream fills.
The waste remains, the waste remains and kills.

ONE ART
Elizabeth Bishop

The art of losing isn't hard to master;
so many things seem filled with the intent
to be lost that their loss is no disaster.

Lose something every day. Accept the fluster
of lost door keys, the hour badly spent.
The art of losing isn't hard to master.

Then practice losing farther, losing faster:
places, and names, and where it was you meant
to travel. None of these will bring disaster.

I lost my mother's watch. And look! my last, or
next-to-last, of three loved houses went.

The art of losing isn't hard to master.

I lost two cities, lovely ones. And, vaster,
some realms I owned, two rivers, a continent.
I miss them, but it wasn't a disaster.

—Even losing you (the joking voice, a gesture
I love) I shan't have lied. It's evident
the art of losing's not too hard to master
though it may look like (Write it!) like disaster.

SLOW POISON

Empson wrote his poem
twenty years before kidney
dialysis was available.
When diseased kidneys
lose the ability to filter out
the wastes that the body
produces, accumulated
waste and poisons shut
down the body's organs
and death occurs. Empson
apparently had read about
an experiment in which
the blood of an old dog,
suffering from kidney
failure, was replaced with
blood from another dog.
He had also heard a rumor
that twenty percent of
China's soil was honey-
combed by tombs, the
dead of earlier generations
occupying land needed by
the living.

ART FROM LOSS

Elizabeth Bishop has no
difficulty purging things—
in fact she has lost far too
much, but she finds in loss
itself material for poetry.

FINAL WORDS

If you have enjoyed this collection of poems to read aloud, you're probably ready to begin your own private collection—one that will grow and deepen over the years. Along the way, like Marianne Moore, you will find much that you don't like, and much that you do. You may ponder, as she does just what poetry is—why words have such power. Perhaps it's because the words become a part of us. In the poem that follows, Tess Gallagher wants to write the voiceless, wordless poem. She puts her "deaf poem" in print understanding that what she wants isn't possible yet. But she knows she gets a little closer every time you make her words your own.

POETRY
Marianne Moore

I, too, dislike it: there are things that are important
beyond all this fiddle.
Reading it, however, with a perfect contempt for it,
one discovers in
it after all, a place for the genuine.
Hands that can grasp, eyes
that can dilate, hair that can rise
if it must, these things are important not
because a

high-sounding interpretation can be put upon them but
because they are
useful. When they become so derivative as to become
unintelligible,
the same thing may be said for all of us, that we
do not admire what
we cannot understand: the bat
holding on upside down or in quest of
something to

eat, elephants pushing, a wild horse taking a roll, a tireless wolf under

a tree, the immovable critic twitching his skin like a
horse that feels a flea, the base-

ball fan, the statistician—

nor is it valid

to discriminate against 'business documents and

school-books'; all these phenomena are important. One
must make a distinction

however: when dragged into prominence by half poets,
the result is not poetry,

nor till the poets among us can be

"literalists of

the imagination"—above

insolence and triviality and can present

for inspection, 'imaginary gardens with real toads in
them', shall we have

it. In the meantime, if you demand on the one hand,

the raw material of poetry in

all its rawness and

that which is on the other hand

genuine, you are interested in poetry.

BOUNDARIES

Moore quotes Leo Tolstoy ("business documents and school-books" are not poetry), W. B. Yeats (William Blake was a "literalist . . . of the imagination," and was so eager to represent the imagination that he discarded useful poetic conventions), and Moore quotes the "imaginary gardens" comment of her friend, poet Archibald MacLeish. The cumulative effect here is of a poem, about poetry, made in part of quotations of prose. If you look carefully you'll notice that this carefully patterned poem often rhymes (eyes/rise, what/bat, etc.). Read out loud, it seems more like a prose argument than verse. Which is exactly the point.

DEAF POEM
Tess Gallagher

Don't read this one out loud. It isn't
to be heard, not even in the sonic zones
of the mind should it trip the word "explosion"
and detonate in the silent room. My love
needs a few words that stay out of
the mouth and vocal cords. No vibrations, please.
He needs to put his soul's freshly inhuman capacity
into scattering himself deeper into
the forest. It's part of the plan that birds
will eat the markings. It's okay. He's not coming
that way again. He likes it where he is. Or if he
doesn't, I can't know anything about it. Let
the birds sing. He always liked to hear them
any time of day. But let this poem meet
its deafness. It pays attention another way, like he
doesn't when I bow my head and press my forehead
in the swollen delusion of love's power to
manifest across distance the gladness that joined us.

Wherever he is he still knows I have two feet
and one of them is broken from dancing.
He'd come to me if he could. It's nice to be sure
of something when speaking of the dead. Sometimes
I forget what I'm doing and call out to him. It's me! How
could you go off like that? Just as things were
getting good. I'm petulant, reminding him of his promise
to take me in a sleigh pulled by horses
with bells. He looks back in the dream—the way
a violin might glance across a room at its bow
about to be used for kindling. He doesn't
try to stop anything. Not the dancing. Not the deafness
of my poems when they arrive like a sack of wet
stones. Yes, he can step back into life just long enough
for eternity to catch hold, until one of us
is able to watch and to write the deaf poem,
a poem missing even the language
it is unwritten in.

SPEAKING TO THE DEAD
Gallagher wrote this poem
after the death of writer
Raymond Carver.

FURTHER NOTES ON THE POEMS

THE PASSIONATE SHEPHERD TO HIS LOVE (PAGE 8)
Marlowe's country come-on plays on the pastoral tradition, but it's not a true pastoral *complaint*—a song of unrequited love.

THE OWL AND THE PUSSY-CAT (PAGE 10)
While pastorals were a carefully cultivated court entertainment, beast fables grew wild as folk songs and tales. These stories of animals that act like people, such as Aesop's fable of the grasshopper and the ant, are often quite ancient and teach a clear moral lesson. Lear's poem, though, is pure whimsy and silliness, part of a Victorian-era fad for nonsense that also produced Lewis Carroll's *Alice's Adventures in Wonderland*.

YE TRADEFUL MERCHANTS THAT WITH WEARY TOIL (PAGE 12)
Spenser's sonnet breaks into three parts: a question (why go so far for treasure?); an observation (my beloved is like treasure); and, finally, a twist (her most precious aspect cannot be apprehended by the eye).

MY MISTRESS' EYES ARE NOTHING LIKE THE SUN (PAGE 13)
Shakespeare wrote his poem after Spenser, and may have had it—or one like it—in mind. Unlike Spenser's *Amoretti*, Shakespeare's collection of sonnets seems to be written to more than one person. This is one of a group written to the "dark lady," a mysterious person about whom scholars have long spec-

ulated. Changes in the language make this poem funnier now than it probably was when it was written, but it was meant to be funny even then. Be careful, though, reading it to your beloved, who may not think the last two lines make up for the rest.

THE SNIFFLE (PAGE 17)

Nash's poem could also be called *doggerel*, a slightly derogatory term used to describe poems with short lines, irregular rhythm, and awkward or repetitive rhymes. Here, though, the rhymes and rhythm are intentionally awkward, which makes them funny.

NON SUM QUALIS ERAM BONAE SUB REGNO CYNARAE (PAGE 22)

Dowson's poem seems pretty tame now, but in its time, at the height of Victorian prudery, it was scandalous. Here, the unfaithful poet, in bed with a prostitute, is tormented by a vision of his love. Compare these sentiments to those courtly lovers of the sonnets you've read. His torment—the pain he punishes himself with—is what allows him to tell her that he has been faithful to her(in his fashion). Pretty kinky stuff.

THE SUN RISING (PAGE 26)

John Donne was the most famous of the seventeenth century "Metaphysical" poets, a group whose poems typically frame a shocking or unusual earthly situation in terms of the universe as they understood it. Here the poet, lying in bed with his lover, is awakened by the sun and (shockingly) begins to insult old Sol, rather than praise him, as is conventional with love poetry.

THEY FLEE FROM ME THAT SOMETIME DID ME SEEK (PAGE 30)

Sir Thomas Wyatt was one of Henry VIII's knights, and at one point was charged with treason following the execution of Anne Boleyn, falling from favor to disgrace. Here he makes a sarcastic observation about the lover who had previously lured him on but now seems interested in other things.

FROM *THE CANTERBURY TALES* (PAGE 90)

The pronunciation and vocabulary of English changed not long after Chaucer's death, which left later poets puzzled about how you were supposed to read his archaic Middle English. Before scholars figured it out in the 1800s, many assumed he was just sloppy. Reading the Middle English is worth the effort: most modern translations sacrifice the sound and rhythm of his language as spoken poetry in order to get the meaning across clearly. But a great poet's meaning is tied inextricably to the way he uses rhythm and rhyme, and Chaucer is no exception. We've used E. Talbot Donaldson's edition of Chaucer, which retains the essence of the Middle English, but makes it somewhat clearer for modern readers. Any good edition of Chaucer will offer a guide to how to pronounce the old words.

GLOSSARY, LINES 1–18

Soote = sweet. *Pérced* = pierced. *Swich* = such. *Vertu engendréd* = flowers are born from the virtue of April's showers. *Zephyrus* = the west wind. *Eek* = likewise. *Holt* = farm. *Ram* = Aries, the constellation in the zodiac where the sun can be found in spring. *Halvé cours yronne* = run half its course. *Yë* =

eyes. *Pricketh* = stimulates. *Hem* = them. *Her corages* = their hearts. *Palmeres* = pilgrims. *Strondes* = shores. *Ferné halwés* = foreign hallowed places. *Couthe* = known. *Holy blissful martyr* = the tomb of St. Thomas á Becket. *Holpen* = helped. *Seke* = sick.

FROM *THE WASTE LAND* (PAGE 91)

Europe was a mess after World War I, and Eliot reflects this in a poem that presents a jumble of images and broken voices. What we're hearing is the death rattle of western civilization. You may find it helpful to consider the poem a snapshot of the mind of Tiresias of Thebes, the legendary seer who could foretell the future. The Greek gods had changed Tiresias from male to female, and back again, and thus the minds and voices of both men and women flicker through his consciousness—several in just this short passage. These are all foreseen by Tiresias, along with bits of the European racial memory. Much of what he sees is a vision of the western world (particularly the financial district of London, where Eliot worked) on April 1, 1921. Confusing? Yes. But Eliot's poem is the single most influential poem of the century, and people are still arguing about it. So it's worth taking the time to puzzle over its complexities.

Starnbergersee = a German lake. *Hofgarten* = a park in Munich. *Bin gar keine Russin, stamm' aus Litauen, echt deutsch* = "I am not a Russian woman at all—I come from Lithuania, a true German." *Marie* = Marie could be any aristocratic Austrian, though Eliot may have had in mind one he knew,

Countess Marie Larish. Who she is isn't really important. Like the rest of the burned-out civilization of postwar Europe, she has fond memories of the past, but the present is something she's trying to escape.

IN MEMORY OF W. B. YEATS (PAGE 92)

Actually, the weather was pretty good the day Yeats died in France. As with the weather report, don't take everything in Auden's poem at face value, particularly the famous line "poetry makes nothing happen": factual instruments and observations (part I) are inadequate for measuring a great poet's passing; biography (part II) is too. Both miss the point. The first two parts attempt to account for his death by scientific and scholarly means, but the third part, in stately, rhymed verse, shows us that only in poetry can we find the true measure of a great poet, the reasons his poems will live on, and the way that they do, in fact, change everything.

MY HEART LEAPS UP (PAGE 102)

Writing about another poem, Wordsworth recalled that in childhood he was filled with "a sense of the indomitableness of the spirit within me," to such an extent that he could hardly admit to the idea that he might die.

WHEN I CONSIDER HOW MY LIGHT IS SPENT (PAGE 112)

Milton went blind about 1651, but went on to compose *Paradise Lost* and other great poems in the next quarter century. This sonnet dates from 1652, and was composed at a time when the epic was taking shape in his mind. Reading it aloud, notice how it differs from those by Spenser and Shakespeare that appear in this book, and don't emphasize rhyme quite so strongly. Lines that are not *end-stopped*—that don't end with a comma, semicolon, period, or seem to end because of their grammar and sense—should be read as if they're a continuous thought with the line that follows. The poetic term for this is *enjambment*.

THE SECOND COMING (PAGE 117)

This was inspired by revolution and turmoil in Yeats's Ireland. Compare it to Blake's "The Tyger"; just as Blake's poem wasn't about a simple tiger, the strange collection of images here—images perceived by the poet in an imaginative "vision"—illustrate something larger that Yeats wants to write about. Here the subject is nothing less than the coming of a new age, much as certain Old Testament prophets foretold the Christian age that dawned in Bethlehem. But this new age—the modern age that seems to be trashing all the old structures and truths by which we understand things—both frightens and thrills the poet.

ODE ON MELANCHOLY (PAGE 131)

Keats's ode begins with a traditional catalog of the accoutrements of Melancholy—black bile—one of the several "humors" (or bodily substances) which, balanced against each other, were believed by medieval doctors to determine temperament in. In Elizabethan times a cult of melancholia was fashionable, and young men at court would affect to be under its influence—writing dark poems, striking somber poses, and so forth. Shakespeare's Jaques, in *As You Like It*, is a good example. Poets in later years often adopted this pose. Keats, writing in the early nineteenth century, suggests that affecting such constant gloom causes one to miss the beauty that comes with true sadness.

DELIGHT IN DISORDER (PAGE 153)

Here's a poet in the sticks who desperately misses life in the big city. If they'd had them then, he would probably have subscribed to all the fashion magazines so he wouldn't fall behind the times. Herrick was forced to leave London for a quiet life as a clergyman in Devonshire. You've probably seen pictures of Elizabethans in their elaborate ruffs and frills. Styles were changing about Herrick's time, and this poem reflects newer ideals of fashion.

Index of Titles